Battle Royal

Nick Stafford's plays include *Bad City* (Half Moon YPT, 1987), *Extra-Ordinary Behaviour* (Half Moon YPT, 1988), *Easy Prey* (Avon Touring, 1989), *The Canal Ghost* (Birmingham Repertory Theatre, 1990), *Back of the Bus* (New Perspectives Theatre Company, 1991), *Moll Cutpurse* (New Perspectives Theatre Company, 1992), *The Snow Queen* (Young Vic, 1992, and Manchester Library Theatre, 1993), *Listen With dA dA (Dreams Invadeth Man)* (Serpentine Gallery, 1993), *The Devil's Only Sleeping* (Cockpit, 1993), *The Go-Between* (Northampton Theatre Royal, 1995), *Grab the Dog* (Royal National Theatre Studio, 1995) and *The Whisper of Angels' Wings* (Birmingham Repertory Theatre, 1997). He has also written for radio and television and won the Dennis Potter Play of the Year Award in 1998.

D0943026

PR
6069
T22B3
1999

NICK STAFFORD

Battle Royal

ff

faber and faber

First published in 1999
by Faber and Faber Limited
3 Queen Square, London WC1N 3AU

Typeset by Country Setting, Kingsdown, Kent CT14 8ES
Printed in England by Mackays of Chatham plc, Chatham, Kent

All rights reserved

Copyright © Nick Stafford 1999

Nick Stafford is hereby identified as author
of this work in accordance with Section 77 of the
Copyright, Designs and Patents Act 1988

This text went to press before the opening night
and may therefore differ from the version as performed

All rights whatsoever in this work are strictly reserved.
Applications for permission for any use whatsoever,
including performance rights, must be made in advance,
prior to any such proposed use, to The Agency,
24 Pottery Lane, London W11 4LZ. No performance may be given
unless a licence has first been obtained

*This book is sold subject to the condition that it shall not, by
way of trade or otherwise, be lent, resold, hired out or otherwise
circulated without the publisher's prior consent in any form of
binding or cover other than that in which it is published and
without a similar condition including this condition being
imposed on the subsequent purchaser*

A CIP record for this book
is available from the British Library

ISBN 0-571-20446-5

2 4 6 8 10 9 7 5 3 1

Characters

Princess Caroline
Mariette, Princess Caroline's companion
Lord Malmesbury
Prince George
Lady Jersey
Maria Fitzherbert
McMahon
Chef
Prince William
Archbishop of Canterbury
The Earl of Jersey
Majocchi
Bartolomeo Pergami
Billy Austin
Louise Demont
Brougham
Denman
Lord Liverpool, the Prime Minister
Lord Chancellor (Speaker)
Gifford
Gangs of Men (Act 3, Scene 3, vii and xvii)
Man (Act 3, Scene 3, vii)
Galdini
Man (off) (Act 3, Scene 6)
Woman (off) (Act 3, Scene 6)
Door-Keeper
Guards Officer
Man 2 (off) (Act 3, Scene 6)
Doctors 1 and 2
Servants
Pugilists

Battle Royal was first performed on the Lyttelton stage of the Royal National Theatre, London, on 9 December 1999, with the following cast:

Mariette Caroline Harker
Princess Caroline of Brunswick Zoë Wanamaker
Lord Malmesbury Hugh Ross
Prince George Simon Russell Beale
Lady Jersey Gemma Jones
Maria Fitzherbert Suzanne Burden
Colonel McMahon Brendan Coyle
Archbishop of Canterbury Colin Haigh
Lord Jersey Martin Chamberlain
Prince William Michael Mueller
Lord Liverpool Patrick Godfrey
Mr Brougham Matthew Macfadyen
Bartolomeo Pergami Duncan Duff
Billy Austin Jay Simpson
Mr Denman William Osborne
Majocchi Benny Young
Louise Demont Valerie Spelman
Galdini Patrick Baladi
Gifford Iain Mitchell
Manservants Patrick Marlowe, Adrian Penketh
Ladies in Waiting Yvonne O'Grady, Janet Spencer-Turner

Director Howard Davies
Designer Rob Howell
Lighting Designer Mark Henderson
Music Paddy Cunneen
Director of Movement Jane Gibson
Sound Designer Adam Rudd
Company Voice Work Patsy Rodenburg

Setting

ACT ONE London, 1795 to 1814
ACT TWO London and Lake Como, 1820
ACT THREE London, 1820

Act One

A palace.
  Enter Caroline and Mariette.

Mariette I am not finished!

Caroline I cannot sit still any more, I cannot sit at all –

Mariette But I am not finished –

Caroline Finish whilst I stand.

Mariette Will you stand still?

Caroline I shall try, but it is almost time –

Mariette And I am not finished, and I must finish.

Caroline And I must pace and I must fidget. Oh my heartbeat, oh my breath – ow!

Mariette If you will not keep still –

Caroline I am trying to!

Mariette Let your mind pace, let your emotions fidget, but keep your person still or I shall prick you more and not be held responsible for your appearance when he first sees you.

Caroline Yes. Good. Here. I am still. No. Still enough? Good. God, help me through this ordeal. Here I am, then. Here we are. In England. Summoned from an outpost. Me. Here I am. See his picture? (*locket*)

Mariette Again. Yes, I look upon it again – keep still!

Caroline 'Here,' said kind Lord Malmesbury, 'this is his portrait.' Isn't Lord Malmesbury a true English gentleman?

Mariette Yes.

Caroline What a land if they all resemble him – which they don't, of course.

Mariette No, they won't. Lift your head.

Caroline Goodbye, mother; goodbye, father. So proud he's chosen me. 'Oh my God!,' my mother said. 'The Prince of Wales seeks your hand? I do not dare to believe.' The line of carriages; goodbye, goodbye Brunswick – goodbye! Head for the sea. This way, that way. A diversion! Napoleon's troops reported over there! Camp here. Wait for escort. Here. Go on. Safe now. To the ship. And Malmesbury, so attentive: 'Perhaps, Ma'am, perhaps I may show you how the Prince conducts himself at the dinner table. Like so. And so. And so.'

Mariette And breathe in.

Caroline And ahoy! ahoy! the white cliffs, and first foot in England. Where's this? Who's that? –

Mariette Be still –

Caroline Be still, be still, both you and Lord Malmesbury tell me be still, and: 'Be dignified, Ma'am, look ahead, be dignified, demure, aloof even.' Aloof? aloof? English words – but they all look at me, they all whisper: where is she? is that her? And I want to shout yes! it is me! here I am! But I am aloof, demure, yes, Lord Malmesbury, I am sorry, Lord Malmesbury – ow!

Mariette Then keep still –

Caroline Ow –

Mariette Still –

Caroline Ow –

Mariette Still –

Caroline Ow! (*joking*) You stab me? The future Queen?

Mariette Not so loud, Ma'am –

Caroline You tell me I am too loud?

Mariette Sssh!

Caroline You almost slay me then you sssh! me?

Enter servants.

Oh dear.

Servant Ma'am?

Caroline A pin, a prick from a pin. I did not mean to be so loud.

Servant Lord Malmesbury is approaching, Ma'am.

Caroline Thank you.

Exit servants.

Oh dear.

Mariette Keep still. Finished.

Caroline Good, for I must go.

Mariette Go?

Caroline I am bursting.

Mariette But Lord Malmesbury will be here in –

Caroline Must go. Bursting. Dangerous. You stay. (*Exits.*)

Enter Malmesbury.

Malmesbury Was that your mistress?

Mariette She will return immediately.

Malmesbury Is she ready?

Mariette Almost, Lord Malmesbury.

Malmesbury Has she chosen wisely? Does she fully look the part?

Mariette Yes.

Malmesbury I cannot over-emphasise the fastidiousness of the Prince of Wales. In matters of personal presentation he exercises minute attention to detail.

Mariette My mistress understands that.

Malmesbury And her perfume, does that complement her dress?

Mariette I have supervised a rigorous toilette.

Malmesbury I know that her intimate details are not my business to –

Mariette My mistress's intimate details are becoming everyone's business, my Lord.

Enter servant.

Servant My Lord, the Prince shall be here in four minutes.

Malmesbury Thank you.

Exit servant.

Then, Mariette, please find and bring her here. And, Mariette, I enjoy your frankness because it has eased my task of bringing your mistress safely here, but may I remind you that most of the English Court would take offence at your lack of deference.

Mariette Yes, my Lord. (*Exits.*)

Enter Mariette. Exit servants.
Enter Caroline.

Caroline Lord Malmesbury.

4

Malmesbury Princess Caroline.

Exit Mariette.

Caroline Have I already done something wrong?

Malmesbury No, no. Everything seems perfect.

Caroline You like my dress?

Malmesbury My taste is completely unimportant –

Caroline You don't like it?

Malmesbury It is an entirely appropriate dress, that is, I suppose, yes, I do like it.

Caroline Good, because you are my guide to the complexities of English manners.

Malmesbury In that case, may I remind your Highness that it is essential you remain calm. Despite the fact you are the most fortunate princess, indeed the most fortunate woman in the world, whose expectations exceed all others, and from whom the world expects great things; despite the excitement your fabulous expectations understandably occasion, it is essential you remain at least outwardly calm.

Caroline Aloof?

Malmesbury Not aloof, no.

Caroline Demure?

Malmesbury Demure is more accurate than aloof. But please, may I take this last opportunity to –

Caroline (*studying a locket*) He is quite handsome, isn't he? A real Hanoverian.

Malmesbury Very much so, and imminently expected.

Caroline As handsome as my father . . . Lord Malmesbury, do not fear. I am a princess, I have grown up in a court. I know that when I am Princess of Wales I must avoid familiarity and remain silent on politics and party. And I shall refrain from asking questions – too many, anyway, I shall have to ask some questions –

Malmesbury Some, of course, yes –

Caroline Such as where is this thing? or who is that person? but I shall refrain from giving opinions, and I shall endeavour to fulfil my duties as future Queen of England. Moreover, as this is a man I am marrying, not just a title, I commit myself wholeheartedly to his personal comfort. I know he has been –

Malmesbury He has an undeserved reputation for enjoying the amusements of his position whilst not embracing the duties; an unwarranted reputation based on isolated incidents which have found their way into the papers –

Caroline I shall domesticate him. I shall inspire in him a relish for home virtues, and he shall be happy.

Malmesbury The nation expects this of you. Do not reproach the Prince, be attentive and soft and endearing –

Enter servant.

Servant The Prince approaches.

Caroline hugs Malmesbury.

Caroline Please, my Lord, remain my protector.

Malmesbury I shall. Dry your eyes. Now, let me see the Princess of Wales. Good. Dignity. Nobility. Charm. Grace. And may I be so bold as to add beauty?

Servant His Royal Highness the Prince of Wales!

Caroline curtsies and stays head down.
  Enter George. He circles her.

George Rise.

They clumsily make contact. She still has her head bowed.

Caroline.

Caroline Your Highness?

Their eyes meet. George retreats as far as he can. Caroline looks to Malmesbury for help.

George Malmesbury, I am not well; pray get me a glass of brandy.

Malmesbury Might I suggest a glass of water?

George Excuse me. (*Exits.*)

Caroline My God! Is the Prince always like that?

Malmesbury No, your Highness. I think he's unwell. I shall seek to –

Caroline I find him very fat, and not as good-looking as his portrait.

SCENE TWO

Carlton House.
  Lady Jersey waits.
  Enter George.

Lady Jersey Very dashing.

George pours himself a large brandy.

George, look to her qualities. I understand she's not too tall, nor too short. They say she's neither fat nor thin; that her teeth are going, but she has good hands. And I hear she has a good bust, and bright eyes.

George Her eyes trouble me.

Lady Jersey Love at first sight is to be hoped for but when it does not happen then you must live with that fact, and hope affection blossoms.

George The expression in her eyes was –

Lady Jersey Was what?

George Wrong, it was wrong.

Lady Jersey Celebrate! Because of this marriage your father approves of you, Parliament is paying off your debts, and the nation is thanking you for giving them an excuse for getting drunk. Your popularity has soared.

George But why is she not married already?

Lady Jersey Probably because she's been living in Brunswick.

George Her father's a fine man, by all accounts.

Lady Jersey And the King likes her mother, so in marrying his sister's daughter you've done something to please him.

George But . . .

Lady Jersey George?

George No. Nothing.

Lady Jersey George?

George Heirs. Children.

Lady Jersey Pretend you are with someone else.

George Yes.

Lady Jersey Think like a wife in a loveless marriage.

George Your marriage isn't loveless, is it?

Lady Jersey No. If I were she, George, I would want to make you as comfortable as possible.

George I don't believe you are envious.

Lady Jersey In order to reassure you, I'm merely explaining how she shall be.

Enter servant.

Servant Your Highness, Mrs Fitzherbert has arrived.

George Oh? Oh. Ask her to wait.

Servant And Lord Malmesbury is here, also.

George Does he know Mrs Fitzherbert is here?

Servant No, sir.

George Maintain his ignorance, and tell him I am indisposed.

Servant He is set upon seeing you, sir.

George Tell him I shall see him as soon as I can.

Exit servant.

Frances, please excuse me.

Lady Jersey Of course. Courage. (*Exits.*)

Enter Maria.
George tries to kiss her.

Maria No.

George Maria.

Maria Cannons are drawn up in the park. The streets are bedecked with flags. I've been trying to think what to do. How to be.

George Yes.

Maria And is it true that Parliament will pay off your debts?

George Is it true?

Maria Is it?

George Yes.

Maria I don't think that having your debts paid for you can be described as 'doing your duty'.

George The discharge of the debts is a side issue, a consequence.

Maria Your dissemblings are so childlike, so easily apprehended.

George Maria, I assure you that Parliament offered to pay off my debts only after I'd agreed to marry.

Maria They offered afterwards? I think not. It appears to me that the discharge of your debts may be the cause of the marriage, and not a consequence, especially, as it seems to me, that you have lied to me.

George Everything I say to you in this matter – I am conscious that every utterance in connection with this matter is hurtful, so if I have omitted details it is to shield you, and myself, from upset. It is my duty to marry, and I cannot deny that I am happy that I shall be relieved of my debts, debts which you, incidentally, have enjoyed contributing to, but the discharge –

Maria I do not make you extravagant.

George That very brooch came from a scoundrel of a jeweller who threatens to publish my debt to him.

Maria Have it back then, return it to him.

George No, I do not want it, it is yours.

Maria Then do not blame me for –

George I do not blame you, but you enjoy being the recipient of presents of precious jewels, you imbibe the finest wines, and you reside in the most modern buildings finished in the most fashionable decor; and I am pursued by jewellers, vintners, builders and decorators who besiege my purse and if I wasn't who I am I'd languish in Fleet debtor's gaol.

Maria So then. She shall be blessed by the Archbishop of Canterbury whereas our furtive union was conducted by an insolvent clergyman whom you persuaded with the promise of a Bishopric.

George Not that he needed much persuading. He needed to get out of gaol and we needed a man of the cloth, no matter how shabby. See, you're almost smiling.

Maria Allow me some bitterness, some jealousy. Would you prefer it if I weren't jealous?

George I wish, I wish so completely that I did not have to –

Maria How much do you owe?

George It's impossible to say until their demands have been rigorously examined.

Maria What is your record?

George Not all these matters are conducted in writing, and the builders, for instance, invariably exceed their estimates, so –

Maria A hundred thousand? More? A hundred and fifty thousand? More? Much more? Two hundred thousand? More? A quarter of a million?

George Your income is what – two thousand a year? If my debts were a quarter of a million, how many years would it take to pay that sum off at a rate of two thousand a year?

Maria One hundred and twenty-five years.

George What year would the debt be discharged?

Maria Nineteen-twenty.

George Well, my probable debt, if one was to pay it off at two thousand a year, would be discharged in the year two thousand one hundred and ten. So, you see.

Maria You must go through with it, then.

George You can see that, can't you?

Maria Yes. I can. You have been very foolish with money.

George But setting aside my debts, I am still expected to marry.

Maria If our marriage is void, then I am a fornicator.

George It is not void. We have our certificate, which I have divided, and placed in two matching lockets, one for you, and one for me, to wear at all times. I have risked my succession for you.

Maria And I have risked excommunication for you.

George Oh, Maria.

Maria Is she pretty?

George No.

Maria And is Lady Jersey her Lady of the Bedchamber?

George Is who, what?

Maria George, you heard and comprehended what I just asked.

George Yes. Yes, Lady Jersey is Lady of the Bedchamber.

Maria Poor Caroline. Look me in the eye and tell me that Lady Jersey is not your mistress.

George Lady Jersey is not my mistress.

Maria Then what is she?

George My friend.

Maria This is all very distressing.

George For us both. Two days after, may I visit you?

Maria I shan't be at home.

George Oh?

Maria I'm going away.

George Can you tell me where?

Maria I'd rather not –

George Go down to Brighton –

Maria No. I'm voyaging overseas.

George Oh?

Maria Tonight. It's the best way I can manage; to make myself entirely absent.

George Can you tell me the date of your return?

Maria The date is when I feel able.

George You are my true wife, Maria, my queen, but you have always known –

Maria I thought, I hoped that you might, I deluded myself that when it came to it, you might simply not do it.

George Please, stay –

Maria I'll wear the locket. (*Exits.*)

Enter servant.

George I'll see Colonel McMahon. Before Lord Malmesbury.

Exit servant. Enter McMahon, unseen and unheard. He studies the Prince before:

McMahon Your Highness.

George Ah. Yes. McMahon. Have someone follow Mrs Fitzherbert.

McMahon Yes, sir.

George She's going overseas.

McMahon Yes, sir.

George Just where, and when, and . . . Everything, really.

McMahon Yes, sir.

George Thank you.

> *Exit McMahon.*
> *Enter a servant.*

Give Lord Malmesbury my apologies. Tell him I am unwell but that I am recovering. Tell him I am very pleased.

SCENE THREE

The nuptial bedchamber.

Caroline So many siblings in such a small chapel. Very hot. Charlotte, Augusta, Elizabeth, Sophia –

> *Enter Lady Jersey. She eavesdrops.*

– Amelia and Mary. Frederick and William. Greetings from Edward in Nova Scotia, Adolphus in Elst, Ernest in Arnheim, and Augustus in Rome.

Mariette Who wore the most beautiful dress?

Caroline Frederick. No, me of course. I've eaten too much. I'd never get into that dress again.

Mariette There shall soon be another cause for an increase in girth.

Caroline I don't know that I'd like thirteen, though. What's this? Yardley's Lavender toilet water. (*Sprays, dabs*). Thank you. And is my breath offensive?

Mariette No.

Caroline It was so hot in the chapel that it boiled the Archbishop of Canterbury's brains; he forgot where he was in the service and said the same thing twice.

Mariette Oh my. What did he say twice?

Caroline 'Any person knowing of a lawful impediment.' He stopped, he completely stopped. And stared.

Mariette Did you want to laugh?

Caroline Yes, but I contained it. George looked as if he might faint away. He had to get up off his knees. Oh. Good evening, Lady Jersey. Thank you, Mariette.

Mariette Goodnight, your Royal Highness. Lady Jersey.

Lady Jersey Goodnight.

Exit Mariette.

Caroline I thought it went terribly well today.

Lady Jersey Didn't it? I thought it quite the best wedding I have been to for some time.

Caroline Well, it should be, shouldn't it? It should be the best wedding since the last time the heir to the throne was married. Their Majesties have been married thirty-five years, have they not?

Lady Jersey They have.

Caroline Were you a guest?

Lady Jersey No.

Caroline How old were you, then?

Lady Jersey It must be a great relief to be married at last.

Caroline Were you a beauty? I never was. Not pretty-pretty. You must share your secrets with me. The unguents and potions that sustain you. Where is Lord Jersey tonight?

Lady Jersey He'll still be celebrating your Royal Highness's immense good fortune, I expect.

Caroline I understand my husband has appointed your husband Master of Hounds. And here you are, Lady of my Bedchamber. My good fortune gives rise to your good fortune.

Lady Jersey All of us within the royal compass are indeed blessed.

Caroline Tell me about him.

Lady Jersey About my husband?

Caroline My husband. You are his friend.

Lady Jersey His manners are impeccable. He can illuminate a room if he chooses just by his personality, regardless of his title. He's clever.

Caroline Why hasn't he married before?

Lady Jersey I have no idea.

Caroline Why does he marry now?

Lady Jersey Because it is now that the heir to the throne makes a suitable match.

Caroline Tell me his flaws.

Lady Jersey His flaws?

Caroline He had been drinking today. He was completely betrunken. Someone had to hold him up.

Lady Jersey Your Highness; I don't think it's proper for me to have this conversation with you.

Caroline Tell me about his debts.

Lady Jersey I know nothing of his personal finances.

Caroline He likes to spend far too much on finery. This makes some people nervous. They are frightened of comparisons with Louis XV.

Lady Jersey But the people demand that he live like a prince.

Caroline A difficult balance to strike. The times are awful and momentous. The French Revolution. Napoleon. The conduct of all the royal families is closely scrutinised. Radicals and Republicans are constantly alert for any opportunity to foment disunity. I don't want you and I to be enemies.

Lady Jersey Why should we be enemies?

Caroline In Brunswick I received a letter. It warned that you are 'the worst and most dangerous of profligate women', 'driven by envy', intent on my 'ruin'.

Lady Jersey May I ask who signed this defamation?

Caroline It was anonymous.

Lady Jersey Then I hope your Royal Highness dismissed it as malicious.

Caroline But you are hostile towards me. Is it envy? I expect envy from other women despite the fact that my title is one which the overwhelming majority are ineligible to occupy.

Caroline strays near a window. Cheers from a crowd outside.

A servant lowers the lights. The crowd makes ribald noises.

Lady Jersey turns down the bed sheets.

Lady Jersey You occupy a position of which nearly every woman dreams, yet none, bar one, can fulfil.

Servants bring food, drink.

Enter George and the gynaecologist.

Exit servants.

George My, my dear . . . Um, this is –

Gynaecologist Good evening, your Highness.

Caroline Yes.

Exit Caroline and gynaecologist.

George This is my last hope.

Lady Jersey In Brunswick she received a letter warning her of me.

George Warning?

Lady Jersey That I envy her and am intent on her 'ruin'.

George A letter from whom?

Lady Jersey Anonymous. And she knows you have debts; that you 'spend far too much on finery'.

George Oh, do I? Married but a few hours and already she criticises me. What are they doing in there?

Lady Jersey George, what about what this letter said of me?

George Denied it, didn't you?

Lady Jersey Yes, but I'm worried who sent it.

George This letter by some meddler seems irrelevant at this moment, teetering as I am on the precipice of –

Lady Jersey Perhaps –

George D'ye think he's found something? Nothing, preferably –

Lady Jersey Perhaps –

George The discovery of the absence of something is highly desirable.

Lady Jersey I think the sender of the letter is not a meddler but someone who cares for you.

George Cares for me?

Lady Jersey A party who cares if you marry.

George Are you referring to whom I think you are?

Lady Jersey The letter also defamed me as 'the worst and most profligate of women'.

George If it was sent by Mrs Fitzherbert it was because she is wounded and –

Enter gynaecologist. He and George have a mute exchange. Caroline is a virgin.

Oh, God. Oh, God.

Enter Caroline, unseen by George and Lady Jersey. She can't hear them.

I cannot do this.

Lady Jersey It doesn't have to be tonight.

George But if not tonight, another night.

Lady Jersey (*to Caroline*) Your Highness.

George Ah, Caroline.

Exit Lady Jersey.

May I pour you a drink?

Caroline Yes, please.

George What would you like?

Caroline I don't know.

George What do you normally like?

Caroline May I have what you have?

George Brandy?

Caroline Yes.

George With a little water?

Caroline Do you take your brandy with water?

George God, no.

Caroline Then neither shall I.

George Very well. (*He pours. He drinks. He paces. He looks to the doors, as if he might flee. He drinks.*) Has everything so far been to your liking?

Caroline Yes, thank you.

George Do you like England?

Caroline What I have seen.

George How did you find Mother?

Caroline She is as gracious as I expected.

George Never puts a foot wrong, never gets involved in anything contentious. Never hear so much as a peep from her except in private. Tell me, what kind of thing do you expect from . . .? What kind of . . .? Your father has a fine reputation as a soldier.

Caroline He's a warrior.

George Useful in a soldier, but not in a wife.

Caroline I have been well schooled in my duties and have no intention of fighting with you. I crave domestic felicity.

George Yes.

Caroline And mutual respect.

George Yes.

Caroline And affection.

George Isn't that the same as mutual respect?

Caroline I shall love, honour and obey you.

George Good. Now, of course . . . One of the duties, a responsibility . . . A manifestation and a cause of the mutual respect and domestic felicity shall be – (*He falls into the fireplace. Caroline helps him up.*) Fell over.

Caroline Are you hurt?

George Not a bit.

Caroline It's a good job the fire's not lit.

George What's funny?

Caroline I said it's a good job the fire's not lit. You would have been burned.

George What's funny about that?

Caroline Nothing.

George I agree.

Caroline May I have another?

George Yes. Good. Another thing about Mother is that, crucially, she is a mother. With my father. I don't mean my father's a mother – did it sound like I did? I mean she's a mother, and he's a father. Yes. So, then. Yes. Forgive me. Am I babbling? Are you hot? Oh – I didn't mean, y'know –

Caroline It is hot in here.

George What? Yes, I am sleepy. Shall we . . .?

They retire behind their respective screens. Discarded clothes appear. He gets into bed. She gets in. They lie apart, shaking.

You see, that's the most important thing about Mother. Us. We, her children. The succession is assured. No one has to worry about what's happening next. Not only was the succession assured, there's lots of us in case anything awful befell me. I mean, if I hadn't married you perhaps Frederick, or William, or Edward, or Alfred might have. No, not Alfred, he's only fifteen, but –

Caroline I'm glad it is you.

George Good. Good. Glad? Really?

Caroline Yes. I'm glad it's you. I'm glad I'm your wife.

George Good. What's your scent?

Caroline Yardley's.

Caroline Yes, I like it.

George Yes.

Caroline Yes.

They slide under the covers.

SCENE FOUR

Nine months later. Caroline is in bed giving birth. Present are Prince William, the Archbishop of Canterbury, the Lord Chancellor, the Lord President of His Majesty's Council, the Duke of Leeds, the Duke of Devonshire, the Earl of Cholmondley, the Lord Chamberlain, the Earl of Jersey, Lord Thurlow – all to verify the baby is the heir to the throne. Also present: the gynaecologist, female servants.

It's been a hard labour and it's a difficult birth.
There's some disappointment on discovering it's a girl.
Exit Lord Jersey.
The child is taken to the windows, held aloft by the Archbishop. Caroline is left alone.

Canterbury Long live Princess Charlotte!

The crowd roars and takes up the cry. Cannons are fired. Fireworks ignited.
Charlotte is returned to her mother.
Everyone's delighted. Exit the Dukes, etc.

SCENE FIVE

Carlton House.

George What's going on outside?

Servant A crowd forms, sir.

Enter Lord Jersey.

George Lord Jersey?

Lord Jersey Your Royal Highness. It is my proud honour to inform you that at ten minutes past nine o'clock this morning Princess Caroline gave birth to a daughter. God save Princess Charlotte!

George Champagne!

Lord Jersey Congratulations, sir.

George Thank you, Lord Jersey. Thank you. Thank you. And the child is healthy?

Lord Jersey She seems very healthy, sir.

George And the mother?

Lord Jersey Well, sir.

Enter servant with message.

Servant From the King, sir.

George (*reads*) 'Congratulations. We are overjoyed at the birth of our first grandchild. Love her as you would a boy. It is no disappointment that the child is a girl. Indeed, I always wished it should be of that sex. I raise a toast to the first of many.'

Enter servant.
   Champagne is opened.

Servant Messages from the Prime Minister, the Archbishop of Canterbury, the Lord Mayor of London, the Prussian Ambassador, the Editor of *The Times*.

George Send for my chef!

Enter William.

William Well done, George, congratulations. Nine months to the day, that gives us all something to aspire to. And she's immense!

George Thank you, William. Thank you.

William Crowds outside. You should go out, give them a wave.

William throws open the windows. The crowd respond.

24

It's you they want, not your brother.

George shows himself. The crowd go wild.

Feels good?

George Feels very good.

William Lifts one up, doesn't it? Bloody, bloody marvellous. (*He silences the crowd.*) I propose a toast, to be echoed throughout the land, in every house, in every tavern, in every church. Let the church bells ring, let the fireworks . . .? (*aside*) What's the word for what fireworks do? What the hell. Let the fireworks firework!

The crowd laugh at his joke.

And let every Englishman cry, 'Long Live Princess Charlotte!'

The crowd reply.
Enter Lady Jersey.
Lord Jersey hands her champagne.

Lady Jersey Your Highness, may I offer my wholehearted congratulations on the successful birth of your daughter.

George Thank you, Frances.

Enter the chef.

Chef On behalf of the kitchen, your Highness, may I offer our congratulations. We look forward to preparing many, many dishes for the Princess Charlotte.

George And today, many, many dishes for my guests. All day. Everything. Excel yourselves.

Exit the chef.

William I'm going to go up to the Palace, George. Well done again. (*Exits.*)

Lord Jersey I also have my duties to perform, but I shall fulfil them with a glad heart.

George Thank you, Lord Jersey.

Exit Lord and Lady Jersey.
Enter McMahon.

Yes?

McMahon Mrs Fitzherbert's in Hammersmith.

George And?

McMahon She still won't see you.

George Did you give her the portrait of my eye?

McMahon Yes, sir.

George And what did she say?

McMahon She turned it this way and that before
identifying it as your right eye.

George And?

McMahon She said it is confirmation that you are
always watching her.

George Oh –

McMahon I think she is still affectionate towards you.

George You think?

McMahon I'm fairly certain. But she won't see you until
she is reassured that following your 'official' marriage it
would not be a sin for her to be intimate with you.

George Reassurance from whom?

McMahon The Pope.

George The what?

McMahon The who, sir, the Pope.

George Then I despair.

McMahon Do not despair, sir; perhaps the Pope will be delighted that the heir to the English throne is married, albeit secretly, to a Catholic, but –

Enter Lady Jersey. McMahon gestures she should stay away. George confirms this; she's furious.

– I have to tell you, sir, that tonight she again voyages overseas.

George Please, McMahon. Please go to her and –

Enter Lord Malmesbury.

Malmesbury Your Highness; this is a wonderful day for yourself and for the nation.

George Yes. The birth gives good reason for great rejoicing.

Malmesbury You have brought joy to the people, provided a welcome distraction from their commonplace woes. May your union be blessed again and again.

George You should have reported her defects.

Malmesbury Defects, sir?

George Yes, defects, sir. In Brunswick, sir, when sent to gain her consent.

Malmesbury If there had been any notorious or glaring or irrevocable defects I would have felt it my duty to state them – but to the King, at whose command I sought the Princess's hand in marriage.

George Do not dissemble, Lord Malmesbury. You must have at least heard something.

Malmesbury I had heard but dismissed the gossip that all was not completely felicitous between your Royal Highnesses –

George From whom and what have you heard?

Malmesbury For instance, you haven't been seen abroad together. You've been mostly in Brighton and she's been –

George How on earth, then, does anybody think we begat a child?

Malmesbury Exactly, sir. The child will dispel any doubts.

George Next time you hear gossip like it, question its provenance, and report it to me.

Malmesbury Sir, I would rather not have to convey every piece of gossip that –

George I order you to bring to my attention any item concerning the Princess Caroline.

Malmesbury With respect, sir, I was and remain the King's envoy –

George Is your presence here now an errand ordered by my father?

Malmesbury No, sir. I thought to –

George Then you are excused.

    Exit Lord Malmesbury.

Lady Jersey More champagne, your Highness?

George And a brandy.

Lady Jersey What has upset you?

George I want to be alone. I said, I want to be alone!

    Exit all, bar McMahon.

Increase the watch on the Princess. Keep watching her. Just . . . Find out things. And intercept Mrs Fitzherbert, persuade her to stay within these shores, tell her that

I love her, tell her that I'll die without her, tell her that she is my true wife, tell her I wish the child was hers, say that to her – no, let me write it!

He exits, followed by McMahon.

Caroline's quarters.

Mariette Where is he today?

Caroline He hasn't informed me, yet.

Mariette Who is coming for dinner, today?

Caroline No one.

Mariette Not even Lady Jersey?

Caroline No one but her.

Mariette Do you know when you shall see him?

Caroline Not certainly.

Mariette Shall it be this week?

Caroline I expect so.

Mariette To the opera, perhaps?

Caroline Perhaps. Mariette, stop it.

Mariette But –

Caroline Stop it. Go away. Go away.

Mariette Yes, Ma'am, I should like to go away. I'd like to return to Brunswick.

Caroline You cannot.

Mariette I humbly request it.

Caroline No –

Mariette You do not care for yourself –

Caroline You cannot –

Mariette You do not dress carefully –

Caroline I forbid it –

Mariette You thwart me in my duties –

Caroline If you go I won't have any friends. Talk to me, Mariette. Tell me about England; what is it like out there?

Mariette Ask your dining partner, she has her liberty. She is seen everywhere. For instance, she is often seen in the company of the Prince of Wales.

Caroline Lady Jersey may be a difficulty, but she isn't *the* difficulty. I even quite like her. I live in someone's shadow but it is not cast by Lady Jersey. If I saw who cast it I'd know her at once. England, tell me about England.

Mariette The war goes on. People starve. The English are scared what might happen if anything befell the King before Napoleon is defeated. They wonder if his eldest son has the, how may I put it? They wonder if he has the –

Caroline You are being indiscreet.

Mariette You asked me to tell you.

Caroline About England. Amuse me with some English words that you will have heard used amongst the servants.

Mariette A man is a 'chap'. A husband is a 'gaffer'. And drunkenness, there are many words for drunkenness: 'stewed to the eyeballs', 'stewed to the gills' and 'stewed as a prune'. Then there are the inebriated conditions: 'addled', 'skunked' and 'rammaged'.

Caroline Addled, skunked and rammaged. Do they denote different degrees of drunkenness?

Mariette Not that I can tell.

Caroline Parts of the body. Words for women's parts.

Mariette 'The name-it-not. The gate of life. Cupid's Alley. The old hat –'

Caroline The old hat?

Mariette Because it is frequently felt.

Caroline Very good. I like that. Now men's parts.

Mariette 'Wedding tackle, crown jewels. Dibble. Dong.'

Caroline Dibble and dong? Marvellous! Dibble. Dong. Do dibble and dong denote different forms of the man's part?

Mariette Yes, a dibble is –

Caroline Don't tell me, let me guess! A dibble is less, how shall I say, less apparent than a dong?

Mariette Yes, yes! I mean, so I am told.

Caroline Now, to curses.

Mariette 'Go to hell with your mother and make a bitch pie.'

Caroline God's truth, goodness me, how eloquent. One should save such a very special curse for an auspicious occasion. I am enlightened. You have cheered me up, Mariette.

Mariette I have assisted in distracting you from that which weighs upon you. He is not beyond reproach – you asked me what it's like out there and I can tell you that he cannot be confident of his popularity because it is apparent that despite the times his flamboyance goes unchecked, and I should not be your only friend –

31

Enter Lady Jersey.

Lady Jersey Your Highness.

Caroline Lady Jersey; does your husband possess a dibble, or a dong?

Lady Jersey Possess what?

Caroline Do you have an old hat? Mariette, what is the matter?

Mariette Nothing.

Lady Jersey I am not familiar with these expressions. You have me at a disadvantage. I know what a hat is, of course –

Caroline Mariette?

Mariette I thought I would sneeze, but it has passed.

Lady Jersey I have interrupted something.

Caroline We fill our time alone together with foolishness.

Lady Jersey Have I perhaps upset you by my unavoidable lateness?

Caroline Are you late? Do you want me to be upset?

Lady Jersey I was detained.

Caroline As I am. Lady Jersey, I believe that whenever I have asked a direct question you have answered truthfully. Of course you never freely offer the truth, but you do answer truthfully to a direct question. The difficulty is finding the question to pin you on.

Lady Jersey I feel at a distinct disadvantage, your Highness, for I have no idea what has provoked this reception.

Caroline A direct question: if you were I, would you expect to live as I do?

Lady Jersey No.

Caroline What would you do, then, if you were I?

Lady Jersey The law is that a wife must obey her husband.

Caroline Do you obey your husband?

Lady Jersey I am obedient.

Caroline You do everything he orders?

Lady Jersey Yes.

Caroline And everything he asks?

Lady Jersey Yes.

Caroline Immediately, without dispute?

Lady Jersey I sometimes seek clarification, but I never proceed as far as disputation.

Caroline And what about matters on which he has expressed no orders or requests; when they arise do you ask yourself what you anticipate his order or request would be, or do you proceed in something until he expressly refers to it?

Lady Jersey Can you be more specific?

Caroline If, for instance, he has never said to you, 'Wife, don't go to Denmark,' if someone suggests to you that you do go to Denmark, do you feel able to go because Lord Jersey has never expressly ordered you not to?

Lady Jersey I have no desire to go to Denmark.

Caroline Mariette. It is cold in here. Would you please fetch more blankets for Charlotte's cot?

Exit Mariette.

You are very entertaining. I can see what good company you must be.

Lady Jersey Yet?

Caroline I wish I could choose your company, rather than have it forced upon me. Another direct question; on my wedding night you said to me: 'You occupy a position of which nearly every woman dreams, yet none, bar one, can fulfil.' You wished me to believe that the 'one' you referred to was yourself, but I think not; who is he in love with? He's told me that he's in love with someone –

Enter servant and Mariette.

Servant Your Royal Highness –

Mariette envelopes Caroline in a cloud of perfume.

– His Royal Highness the Prince of Wales requests to see you.

Caroline Can you ask him to wait?

Servant I can try, Ma'am. (*Exits.*)

Caroline What's this?

Mariette Lubin's Eau de Cologne, No. 4711.

Caroline (*urgently checks her appearance*) You may go.

Exit Lady Jersey, Mariette.
Enter George.

George Ma'am.

Caroline Sir.

George Are you well?

Caroline Yes, sir. And delighted by this unexpected visit.

George Do you have any complaints you wish to draw to my attention?

Caroline All my thoughts have been fixed on looking forward to our next time together.

George You speak like a dutiful wife.

Caroline And behave as one, I assure you.

George I think not.

Caroline Sir, if I have offended through ignorance of English etiquette then I beg forgiveness. Cut off as I am from society, my ignorance is genuine and natural –

George So you do have a complaint.

Caroline Not a complaint, sir. I believe you have had affairs of state to attend to and perhaps these have occupied you so greatly that my circumstances have slipped your mind.

George And instead of approaching me through the authorised channels you chose a devious route. (*He shows her a headline in* The Morning Post.) 'Is the Princess of Wales a state prisoner?'

Caroline Is who?

George You, you.

Caroline Me?

George Are you a prisoner?

Caroline Me?

George Yes, you.

Caroline Am I the Princess of Wales? Yes, yes! I am aren't I? I do dimly remember being a princess –

George Very witty –

Caroline 'The Lost Princess' –

George Very droll –

Caroline Or 'The Ghost Princess of Carlton House'.

George Very impudent.

Caroline I'm trying to make light of the article.

George Too late. By leaking this to a Tory paper knowing they are against me you have involved yourself in politics –

Caroline I did not 'leak' it –

George Yes you did, and they ran it in the same edition as this scurrilous item about that jeweller who says I owe him –

Caroline Sixty thousand pounds?

George Who is your messenger?

Caroline I only see Lady Jersey, your friend whom the first article slurs.

George I know that Lady Jersey is not your messenger.

Caroline But then, perhaps it isn't a slur, for it only says she has been seen at the same places as you – unlike my-self – and that you are friends. But whatever it implies it is not 'leaked' by me via some 'messenger', it is speculation based on observing our absence from society.

George In order that we should make our situation –

Caroline Situation? –

George Marriage, as tolerable to each other as is possible, no more slanders like this can appear in the public papers –

Caroline Then we must appear happy together –

George Appear happy, yes –

Caroline Appear content –

George Avoid discontent or unhappiness, yes. Be content with the cards fate has dealt us.

Caroline What cards does my husband think that fate has dealt me?

George You are Princess of Wales and if I succeed my father you shall be Queen of England, and you have a bonny daughter. I think most people would agree that's a pretty good hand. Don't you agree that that's a pretty good hand?

Caroline It is an incomplete hand.

George But if one plays it right, one can't lose, can one?

Caroline Would you dine with me today?

George I have an appointment.

Caroline Can you not face dining with me? We live in the same house yet I never see you. You hardly look into my eyes. I fear that the way it is described in this public paper is how it is and how you prefer it to be, and all that irks you is that it is known.

George I am not irked, I am outraged! You attempted to rally support for your cause –

Caroline What 'cause'? –

George Listen! –

Caroline What cause? Support from whom? From where? I am nothing here but through you. I have hardly seen the country and I know almost none of its inhabitants. Like your mother, I shall always distance myself from politics, and –

George Is my mother your model? Then you haven't studied her well. She promotes the King's comfort without complaint.

Caroline My complaining, which you complain of, my complaining that does not exist but only in your head; in your complaining of my complaining you reveal you expect me to complain, you anticipate it because you know it to be justified.

George My mother has never talked to my father like this!

Caroline If you require me to resemble your mother then it is reasonable to expect that you resemble your father.

George For God's sake!

Caroline Shall you be my husband? Your mother has thirteen children yet I only have one.

George And what shall she grow up like? Imagine thirteen like you!

Caroline What is it? – who? What or who causes you to treat me in this way?

George You know my wishes, so if you transgress the fault lies with you! (*Exits.*)

Caroline has a (minor) temper tantrum.
Enter Mariette.

Mariette Ma'am, the Prince has said that the Princess Charlotte is not to be brought to you today.

Caroline Is she unwell?

Mariette He did not say, Ma'am.

Caroline What ails her?

Mariette He did not say, Ma'am.

Caroline Shall I see her tomorrow?

Mariette He did not say, Ma'am. I have related the message in its entirety.

UNIVERSITY OF WINNIPEG, 515 Portage Ave., Winnipeg, MB. R3B 2E9 Canada

DISCARDED

Caroline Thank you . . . No. I shall not apologise.
Should I? No. Do we apologise to Napoleon when he
provokes us? I shall dictate a letter. Dear Uncle George,
when considering your eldest son do you find from time
to time that it enters your head the question how on
earth did I begat that? No, no. Too informal. Dear
Father-in-law. No. Your Majesty? Yes, yes. 'Your
Majesty, etc. etc. It has been made known to me that
rumours which damage your Majesty's family and
discredit the crown are appearing in the public papers,
affording opportunity for those mischievously opposed
to the crown to foment disharmony, and threatening
the happiness hitherto enjoyed by the Prince of Wales
and me. I hold no personal grudge against Lady Jersey,
but in the hope of resolving this difficult situation I am
offering to agree to her release before the weight of
public opinion goes too much against us. Your humble
servant etc. etc.' See it delivered. Now, before I cool.

Mariette If you are sure, Ma'am.

Caroline Take it!

Exit Mariette.

SCENE SEVEN

George's apartments.

George She is returned to England?

McMahon She had to go the long way around, sir. Two
of Napoleon's armies were in the way.

George Damn Napoleon.

McMahon I shouldn't take it personally, sir. I don't
think delaying Mrs Fitzherbert's return to these shores
was a conscious part of his strategy.

George How is she disposed toward me?

McMahon I think she may have given in to her feelings for you but then she saw this. (*The Morning Post.*)

George And that set her against a reconciliation?

McMahon I think that tipped her. Eighteen months, sir, is not long for a woman to be angry.

George Is she angry, or is she merely sulking?

McMahon I'd credit her with angry, sir.

George But the Pope blessed her.

McMahon He did.

George Are you Catholic?

McMahon No, sir.

George One of us, then.

McMahon My mother is, sir, but my father's not so I have elected to be neither. But I understand how hard it must be for Mrs Fitzherbert that you are the next head of the Church which persecutes her faith.

George You make it sound as if she condescends to me when surely it is the other way around? I have overlooked her faith because I love her.

McMahon See now, sir. I'm getting a nasty feeling of *déjà écoute*, because that's precisely the kind of thing my parents would argue.

George Has she set any conditions?

McMahon Not as such, sir. But I do have the feeling she would feel humiliated to return to you at a time when there is so much public interest in you, the Princess of Wales, and Lady Jersey.

George Has she said as much?

McMahon No, sir. She does not speak outright. She has her intuitions and I have to guess what they are. I think another woman would be the best to send to her, someone who talks the same tongue.

George Colonel McMahon; you do not think this matter is worthy of your attention.

McMahon It is not work I am accustomed to.

George But does it have your full attention?

McMahon I fulfil all my tasks to the best of my ability.

George But you'd rather be hiding in dark places, armed to the teeth, prepared to ambush spies and conspirators.

McMahon Hitherto that has been my lot.

George This work is as important. You are the only man I trust. When I am King I shall depend on you as much as I do now, John. More, even.

McMahon I am honoured, your Majesty.

George Yes. So, in the tavern, when your friends boast of their martial exploits, do not be envious. Remind yourself of the importance of your commission, and smile at your prospects.

McMahon Yes, sir.

George So, the article in *The Morning Post* has tipped her away?

McMahon She seems to think Lady Jersey has undue influence over you.

George She has said that outright?

McMahon Not to me, sir.

George To someone else?

McMahon I don't know if Mrs Fitzherbert has said it to anyone, but someone has said it to someone, for it is abroad.

George It is abroad that I do Lady Jersey's bidding?

McMahon Yes.

George Do you think that if I were to distance myself from Lady Jersey it would enhance the possibility of a full reconciliation with Maria?

McMahon It might be wise to attempt it as a tactic, sir. To test it, as it were.

George What do they say of Lady Jersey?

McMahon Public opinion, sir? On the one hand she is a beautiful, elegant woman, whose true friendship with your Royal Highness is deliberately misconstrued by your enemies; whilst on the other hand she is a manipulative bitch who has plotted and whored her way up to a position she could not have expected to achieve by legitimate means. Sir.

George Do you know anything detrimental to the owner of *The Morning Post*?

McMahon Not yet.

Enter servant.

Servant Your Highness, Lady Jersey is here.

George John, can you wait outside a while?

McMahon Sir.

George No. Go out where Lady Jersey enters.

McMahon Sir.

Enter Lady Jersey. McMahon passes her. She recognises this as a bad sign.

George Frances, it's terrible.

Lady Jersey What is?

George This whole business.

Lady Jersey What business?

George If I remember rightly, it was from your lips that Caroline of Brunswick's name first fell.

Lady Jersey I'm sure you were aware of your cousin's existence before I might have mentioned her.

George I knew she was alive, but I recall it was you who suggested I marry her.

Lady Jersey I only recall that you said you had to marry, and I helped you make your selection.

George Are we quarrelling?

Lady Jersey I have arrived to find you disposed that way.

George And no fault lies with you?

Lady Jersey You are implying it is my fault that you are married to Caroline.

George Not your fault, Frances, but you influenced my decision, did you not?

Enter servant.

Servant Your Royal Highness, Prince William and Lord Malmesbury seek an audience.

George I expect they do. Show them in.

Exit servant.

You haven't read *The Morning Post*, have you?

Lady Jersey No?

George Take it with you.

Exit Lady Jersey.
  Enter Prince William and Lord Malmesbury.

William. Lord Malmesbury.

William Father has commissioned us to –

George Tell him I've seen the two pieces and I utterly refute everything. I've discussed the one with my wife, and as for the second that jeweller is a well-known fraud and scoundrel.

William We are not here solely on account of the items in *The Morning Post*.

George Oh?

William May we sit?

George Of course.

William Lord Malmesbury, you are probably better at this sort of thing than I.

Malmesbury Very well. His Majesty has commissioned us to convey his reactions to a correspondence he is in receipt of. This is a copy.

With increasing disbelief, George reads it.

William Would you like a brandy, George?

George Thank you, William.

William Father will write to Caroline that she should do her best to make your home agreeable and that parents should avoid disunion for the sake of their little ones.

George What would Father do if Mother wrote such a letter?

William He says to you that whatever has passed between you, you should call a halt to it and endeavour to create another child as soon as possible.

George Would either of you respect a wife who went behind your back?

Malmesbury His Majesty does not condone her actions but being made cognisant of the situation he feels he must intervene.

William He's not saying you must submit to her, but that she must submit to you.

Malmesbury She must submit to you but you must issue wise instructions.

William Sorry to bang on about this, George, but do the letter and the article amount to the truth of the situation? For instance, George, is it true that the Princess is alone a great deal with Lady Jersey?

George In my absence I know not what she does.

William She's only the other side of the house, George.

George Within her own apartments, as befits her station.

William Do you dine with her, or does she dine with Lady Jersey?

George I'd rather see toads and vipers crawl over my victuals than sit at the same table with her. I am sure that she placed that article in the *Post*. The rumours that I treat her badly emanate from her.

William Whatever, Father's sanctioned the dismissal of Lady Jersey.

George Without consulting me? With no proofs of wrong-doing?

William He says the rumours are strong enough to warrant this.

George Won't sacrificing Lady Jersey merely confirm the rumours?

William Father's eager that in cases where there is any doubt we are seen to act. On our journey here we witnessed daubed on a wall 'No Lady Jersey'.

George So, Lady Jersey is sacrificed to public opinion.

William Also, on becoming aware of the articles in *The Morning Post*, Lord Jersey went to Father and vehemently denied the rumours about his wife. Apparently, he pleaded and he begged, which lapse in dignity added to Father's vexation. So Lord Jersey is no longer your Master of Hounds.

George Thank you, gentlemen. Please reassure His Majesty that my first responsibility in all these matters has been and shall continue to be his good name.

Malmesbury Your Highness.

George William. Stay a minute.

Exit Malmesbury.

William, why does Father hate me?

William He doesn't hate you. You are chalk and cheese. I think he is coming to accept your differences, but I think he wishes you would appear to be a sober and responsible heir to the throne. Offer an olive branch, give her another child.

George If offering an olive branch was all one had to do to get her with child I would be the happiest man on earth.

William It can't be that bad.

George It is. She is an antidote to lust.

William For all our sakes, George, take a hold.

George Of her? Around her throat, perhaps.

William I'm being serious.

George Yes, younger brother.

William Well listen, because Father sent me to you rather than ordering you to him. *Vis à vis* that jeweller, Father reminds you that your previous debts were met on your marriage, a singular remedy to which you may have no further recourse. Good luck.

George Thank you, William.

Exit William.

Little prince next-in-line.

Enter McMahon.

Increase the watch on the Princess of Wales and instigate stories to her detriment.

McMahon Such as?

George Have you found nothing?

McMahon Nothing conclusive.

George No inference, no nugget, no seed from which we can propagate suspicions?

McMahon Her aunt Elizabeth of Russia was locked up by Frederick the Great after she refused to live with him.

George Elizabeth of Russia is also my aunt.

McMahon It could be implied that the deviant strain only follows the female line.

George Is it true that two of her three brothers are classed as idiots?

McMahon I strongly suggest that it would be unwise to attempt to disparage the character of the King's niece by drawing attention to the madness alleged to inhabit the King's nephews. The biter could be bit, sir.

George Whatever, please let it be known to Mrs Fitzherbert that Lady Jersey is dismissed. And find something, anything detrimental to the owner of that *Morning Post* rag. That's all now, thank you.

McMahon Sir.

George The most pressing item is, of course, Mrs Fitzherbert.

McMahon Yes, sir. (*Exits.*)

    Enter servant.

George Please ask Lady Jersey to join me.

    Enter Lady Jersey.

Frances. A drink?

Lady Jersey No.

George Bad news, I'm afraid. The King has released you from the Royal Household.

Lady Jersey 'Released' me.

George I argued the path chosen by His Majesty would confirm the malicious gossip, but Caroline has written to him requesting your removal from her proximity.

Lady Jersey When we talked a few minutes ago you were preparing me for this. You were trying to blame me for Caroline, then I read this article and I knew you were telling me, in a rather cowardly way, that I am no longer in favour.

George I would rather this already painful interview did not descend into acrimony.

Lady Jersey Did you tell her you are in love with someone?

George Of course I did not.

Lady Jersey She says you did. She sports with us.

George The King has decreed –

Lady Jersey She is being allowed to set us against each other.

George There is nothing I can do about your dismissal.

Lady Jersey If you hadn't been so foolishly unkind to her she would not have retaliated.

George Perhaps. I regret that I also have to inform you that after Lord Jersey became cognisant of that article in *The Morning Post*, your husband exasperated the King by presenting himself in an agitated state to plead your innocence; hence he is also released.

Lady Jersey At least he is honourable.

George We shall have to look at the possibility of a pension.

Lady Jersey I don't think I am quite ready for a pension.

George I shall do all I can.

Lady Jersey Do you understand, do you have any inkling of what being 'released' means to us?

George It is regrettable.

Lady Jersey Regrettable?! Do you imagine that a pension will meet our needs? Our debts? As soon as it is known we are 'released' from the Royal Household our creditors will descend like carrion crows to –

George Go out with grace, Frances. You've been beaten at your own game.

Lady Jersey You are a scoundrel.

George And you are a bitch, so we have no cause to recriminate each other. Frances; you've had a good long ride on the royal merry-go-round, but now it's spinning too fast for you, you're a bit dizzy and it's time to get off. For a while, maybe not for ever, but for now.

Exit George. Exit Lady Jersey another way.

SCENE EIGHT

Carlton House. Caroline's apartments.
  Enter Lady Jersey.

Lady Jersey I thought the plot would continue for some time –

Caroline Plot? –

Lady Jersey But your letter guillotined it, as it were.

Caroline I hope you and your husband are not severely inconvenienced –

Lady Jersey Oh no –

Caroline I sincerely hope it. Shall we be able to be friends?

Lady Jersey Shall we?

Caroline As long as it doesn't annoy the Prince, of course. I'd like us to be at least amicable.

Lady Jersey Is it true that when you were young you were forbidden to go anywhere without a governess?

Caroline That was true for a while.

Lady Jersey Why?

Caroline Why do you ask?

Lady Jersey Your resilient spirit reminds me of stories I have heard about you.

Caroline I danced too vigorously. Whenever there was a ball I was kept in the next room and only allowed into the ballroom for the more sedate dances, with my governess as my partner.

Lady Jersey And it is reported that you are known to have hysterics.

Caroline Indeed I am. (*She has hysterics, then roars with laughter.*) My parents subdued me until I needed to explode. Once, when there was a ball downstairs I was not allowed to go to at all, I feigned childbirth so convincingly the servants went to fetch my parents. I was only –

Lady Jersey Sixteen. You had put white paint on your face which, when your parents entered, you wiped off as you leapt up crying: 'Now forbid me to go to a ball again!'

Caroline Yes. Yes, that is how it was. From where did you learn the stories about me?

Lady Jersey Oh, around and about. You know what gossip is.

Off, a baby cries.

Caroline Is that Charlotte?

Enter Mariette with a baby.

Mariette I am sorry, Ma'am. It isn't your daughter, but a boy found in the laundry.

Caroline A boy?

Mariette He had this tied to his ankle.

Caroline Billy.

Mariette It appears to be that name.

Caroline In the laundry?

Mariette Yes, Ma'am.

Caroline Let me hold him. There, there. There, there.

Exit Mariette.

You have several children, do you not?

Lady Jersey Nine.

Caroline Nine?

Lady Jersey Seven daughters and two sons. All my husband's, too.

Caroline Oh, I wasn't thinking, I wasn't about to suggest –

Lady Jersey They are all his.

Caroline Such numbers. We'll see.

Lady Jersey Do you anticipate more children?

Caroline Everyone expects it, the birth of royal children – any children – always gives cause for celebration. Do you think this boy is abandoned?

Lady Jersey You were going to ask me who the 'one' is, weren't you? She's a widow. A Catholic widow. Her name is Mrs Maria Fitzherbert. He loves her.

Caroline So does my father 'love' his mistress?

Lady Jersey Maria Fitzherbert isn't George's mistress any more than I am. Ten years before George married you, he married Maria Fitzherbert.

Caroline Married? Married? Is this known?

Lady Jersey The only people who know for certain are the people rumoured to have been present: her uncle, her brother, a clergyman, and of course the happy couple.

Caroline Are there any children?

Lady Jersey None known.

Caroline Is this the truth? Is this the truth?

Lady Jersey It is true that the existence of the marriage is widely believed.

Caroline I must be a laughing stock. An illegal marriage. Does he love her so much?

Lady Jersey I understand that when at first she refused him, he stabbed himself.

Enter servant.

Servant Ma'am –

Enter George, brushing past the servant.

George Lady Jersey? Did you bring my daughter here?

Caroline This is not Charlotte.

Exit Lady Jersey.

George Then who is it?

Caroline Billy. A little boy found in the laundry. I wish it were Charlotte in my arms.

George Why was Lady Jersey here?

Caroline To say goodbye.

George You shall go to Blackheath for the summer.

Caroline Where is Blackheath?

George Over there. Above Greenwich, view of the river.

Caroline Charlotte and I to Blackheath, then.

George She shall visit you there as she visits you here. It rather depends on you. On your understanding of the situation.

Caroline Then Blackheath is a punishment.

George You shall prefer it there. The public papers shall leave you alone instead of fomenting mischief. You would not like others to use you in furthering their own ambitions.

Caroline No, I sincerely would not.

George Good. I would like us to try to be amicable.

Caroline I would welcome that.

George Good. Excellent.

Caroline Were you married already?

George What?

Caroline Before me?

George You are incorrigible!

Caroline Is it true?

George Your imagination runs wild.

Caroline I didn't imagine it, I was told.

George If you were told by Lady Jersey, she whispers poison in your ear because you have dispossessed her.

Caroline Is it true? – it is too fantastic to be a lie.

George I harbour no implacable animosity towards you, Caroline, but neither do I require, or need, or deserve you to maintain any passionate affection toward me. Please do not study me in that way. Our duties are to appear content, and to care for our daughter. Beyond those duties, I can see no necessity for, or occasion in which either of us should make further demands. Shall you be able to fulfil your duty? . . . Caroline, this is important, this is the crux of us . . . Are you able to control your character? . . . Will you speak? . . . Very well. At Blackheath you shall practise appearing content until such time as it shall be proper for our daughter to visit you. (*Exits.*)

Enter Mariette.

Mariette Shall I take him, Ma'am?

Caroline No. Yes.

She has a major tantrum. Billy cries. She finishes her tantrum and takes him back.

I think he's hungry. Bring the food here. I shall feed him.

Mariette Ma'am?

Caroline Billy's abandoned, isn't he?

Mariette We cannot be sure, yet.

Caroline But it looks that way. Shush now, shush. Bring some of Charlotte's food. And her cot.

Mariette Very well. (*Exits.*)

Caroline Shush now. Shush. Food coming. I'll hold you. Billy. Billy. That's a nice name. Shush now.

Act Two

SCENE ONE

1820.
   George, Maria and William at dinner.
   McMahon stands by George, feeding him papers to sign.

George So I said to him, 'Lord Liverpool, how much stoicism would you be able to muster if you were in my position? If your wife had been so ungovernable that to get her out of the way you'd agreed that she should voyage abroad on a fat income, then, when your father died and you inherited – even whilst you mourned your father – you were plagued by speculations that she was planning to return and once again plunge your life into the waters of misery? If you were I, Lord Liverpool – forget that I am King, and set aside that you are Prime Minister' – that sent a shiver down his spine, for he adores being Prime Minister and would hate to be set aside – 'setting aside our stations, if we were the humblest men on earth, we would be forgiven the anxiety occasioned by the possible return of such an errant spouse. As Regent I stoically tolerated her misdemeanours, but as King it is imperative that I and my country are respected and shown due dignity, therefore understand it is necessary that you support me in my desire to be divorced from her.'

William And what did Liverpool reply?

George That he would have to consult his peers. So I said that whilst he was doing that I would continue to consult my advisers *vis à vis* my new government. I know that he fears there's plenty of other Tories who'd jump at the chance to usurp him as Prime Minister –

William Who? –

George But when Colonel McMahon approached – informally – the two leading candidates, both said they couldn't contemplate stepping into Lord Liverpool's shoes in such circumstances.

McMahon Informally, they said that if the precedent was established that the Prime Minister was replaced each and every time he appeared to differ from the King, we should show ourselves to be no better than the uncivilised nations.

George But Colonel McMahon was only sounding out if they'd theoretically step into the Prime Minister's shoes, so of course they said no, in theory, but in practice, if it came to it I've no doubt that they'd usurp him.

Maria George, did you ask Colonel McMahon to informally approach any Whigs?

George No.

Maria You no longer favour any of the Whigs?

George The Whigs are an essential, vital element in our nation's health in that they demand rigorous explanation from the government, but they are not the –

Maria Isn't it strange to be a Whig until you are King, then –?

George I wasn't *a* Whig –

Maria You favoured them –

George No, the Tories favoured my father, so I was a Whig by default –

Maria So you were a Whig? –

William It's just part of growing up, isn't it? When one is young, when one is free to be irresponsible, one deliberately flirts with ideas which antagonise the established order – the established order being Father – then when one matures and takes adult office, one has to have due regard for what is one's duty, rather than one's amusement.

Maria Then if your father had been a Whig, you would have been a Tory? –

George Probably –

William Imagine Father a Whig! –

Maria And a Whig now you are King?

George The Tories are the natural party of government.

William I take it you are a Whig then, Mrs Fitzherbert?

Maria Not *a* Whig.

William But a supporter of the party most likely to emancipate your Faith? Protestant country, I'm afraid. I don't suppose there will ever be a time when a Catholic sits on the throne again. Not in our lifetimes, anyway. No more likely than a Protestant becoming Pope.

Maria The Pope is head of a church, the King is head of a nation; you are not comparing like with like.

George For all you know, William, I could as we speak be signing an invitation to the Pope to attend my Coronation.

William That's not really very funny, George.

Enter a servant.

Servant Your Majesty, Lord Liverpool is here.

Exit Maria. George catches up with her.

George Maria, my duties weigh heavily upon me.

Maria I think your brother dislikes me. Or perhaps he belligerently adopts his new role of heir to the throne, and deliberately antagonises the established order. (*Exits.*)

George Send him in.

Exit servant.

McMahon? – Quickly, aide memoire.

McMahon Maintain his anxiety regarding the security of his position. He will be aware of his rivals.

George Yes. Thank you.

McMahon Charm him, but be forthright and rigorous, he likes argument. (*He conceals himself.*)

William Saw our niece, Victoria, the other day. Walking. Marvellous. Wraps everyone around her little finger. Women, you know; even at that age they know exactly what they're doing. I think you know what I mean.

George You think Mrs Fitzherbert uses me in a cause?

William Everyone tries to influence us, George, it's the way of the world. Are you fully informed of those she passed the time with whilst on her jaunts overseas?

Enter Lord Liverpool.

Liverpool Your Majesty.

George Lord Liverpool.

Liverpool Prince William.

William A drink?

George And a seat; please.

Liverpool Thank you. Port, please. Thank you.

George You have consulted your Peers?

Liverpool I have, and I am mandated to request clarification on certain points. Which are – shall I proceed?

George Please do.

Liverpool Please understand that these enquiries are not necessarily my own. So. Firstly. Is it your position that it would be intolerable to have any, even superficial, purely for the sake of public appearances, any relations with –

George Intolerable, yes. Divorce, yes, that is my position.

Liverpool I cannot shift the Archbishop of Canterbury from his opposition to divorce. He is unable to progress beyond the fact that you are the head of the Church of England, therefore divorce is an anathema. Moreover, he has brought my attention to the legal fact that the alleged adulterous behaviour having taking place in a foreign country cannot be the subject of a trial in a court of this land; and that the man with whom reports say she has an intimate relationship, not being of this nation –

George The man with whom she disgraces her title –

Liverpool Eyewitnesses, do you have eyewitnesses?

George We have a mass of eyewitness statements –

Liverpool Who have seen – there is no delicate way of asking this – who have witnessed them *in flagrante delicto*?

George No, not actually, but in all circumstances, before and after, there is an indisputable narrative that that is what occurs. If a man is seen outside a house holding a knife then is seen entering the house then egressing the house but now the knife is bloody and a body is discovered murdered in the house, stabbed, what would you confidently surmise had happened?

Liverpool Yes, I accept there is a substantial body of circumstantial evidence.

George Thank you.

William Another port?

Liverpool Thank you. The Archbishop of Canterbury is concerned that you have already ordered her name to be removed from the liturgy –

George Yes?

Liverpool In advance of any proceedings –

George He won't allow any proceedings, so what should we do, nothing? Should she be prayed to?

Liverpool There is some concern, given the volatile reputation of the Princess, that to provoke her may not be wise –

George I provoke her? She who travelled to the Holy Land at the head of a bizarre entourage and rode into Jerusalem on an ass?! What does the Archbishop make of that action?

Liverpool That was indeed a strange and provocative action – blasphemous, even – but not grounds for divorce. I have been requested to ask you . . . it is being asked whether you intend to re-marry?

William Metternich; didn't he mention something about a daughter of Victor Emmanuel of Sardinia? You see, Liverpool, she'd be great-great-granddaughter of Charles the First. Thus the Hanovers marry the Stuarts. That'd be good for the country, wouldn't it?

Liverpool I am conversant with the royal lineage, Prince William. It is all our desires that the monarchy is stable, fruitful and popular.

George And it is our desires, in the first instance, that the monarchy is restored to dignity, and that monarch and prime minister are seen to be working in harmony. I have heard that all is not well within your party, that you have rivals.

Liverpool Your Majesty may possess some intelligence that I do not.

George That is all I have heard; that you have rivals.

Liverpool One must expect that. You cannot be swayed against divorce?

George No.

Liverpool Then, mindful that we are responsible both to you and to the nation, I may be able to hatch a compromise, which mention of an ass brings to the forefront of my mind. As with an obdurate ass, so with an obdurate woman – a carrot and a stick. There can be no trial for adultery if the offence is committed on foreign ground – however, there is a Bill which may be brought before Parliament, a Bill of Pains and Penalties which could be brought against her should she dare to return – that is the stick.

George What does this Bill state?

Liverpool That she has committed adultery and must be stripped of her titles.

George And divorce?

Liverpool If the Bill were passed –

George If?

Liverpool When the Bill were passed, then would be the time to say to the Archbishop: 'Look at what has been found – I must divorce her!' Divorce is natural justice once the Bill is passed.

George So, this Bill is the stick, and what is the carrot?

Liverpool I propose we offer an increase in her annual annuity from £35,000 to £50,000, in return for her promise to stay overseas.

George Just that? The only condition is that she stay away?

Liverpool For the time being. Then, at the appropriate moment in the future, if and when you are certain you wish to legitimately re-marry and –

George Did you just stress 'legitimately'?

Liverpool Not intentionally, your Majesty.

George I thought I heard you stress the word 'legitimately' in the same way that I earlier thought you stressed the word 'circumstantial', as in the evidence against Caroline. William; did you hear the Prime Minister place an undue stress on the word 'legitimately'? –

William I couldn't tell –

George Or 'circumstantial'? –

William To say the evidence against her is 'circumstantial' is to belittle her crimes –

Liverpool The thinking behind keeping her out of the country is the level of unpopularity your Majesty unjustly enjoys. And yes, I do stress 'unjustly'. With the French misadventure, then the attempts to copy it here at Peterloo and other criminal gatherings large in the minds of the people, the government entreats you to do absolutely nothing – for the time being – which may foment further unrest. So leave her in Italy, we shall pay her to stay away, she cannot want to return and be shamed more than she already is. Offer the carrot of £50,000 a year to stay away, and threaten the stick of the Bill of Pains and Penalties in the unlikely event of her return. Politically, this is by far the wisest course to steer, it allows us to adjust our position in response to changing conditions and does not preclude any future remedy, including divorce – which I support – but don't tell Canterbury I said that.

George Thank you, Prime Minister. My instinct is to be favourable towards your proposition, but I need time to consider it. Just tonight. No, actually, could you wait outside for a few minutes?

Liverpool Certainly. (*Exits.*)

George William?

William Good.

George Colonel McMahon?

McMahon I'd accept. It's an efficient compromise, and he's right, the evidence against her is inconclusive, so I'd like to go to Italy.

George Go, then.

    Exit McMahon.

Ask the Prime Minister to return. I signed a thousand papers today.

William Did you read them all?

George God, no.

William Lady Herford's having a party tonight. She asked me to mention it to you.

George I shall mention it to Mrs Fitzherbert.

William I'm not sure Lady Herford would want you to do that.

George Then I shan't, and I shan't attend.

William You must be careful who you are seen about with. As we all should. Ask Mrs Fitzherbert about the

Marquis de Bellois. Ask her if it's true that he's the handsomest man in France. The Marquis be Bellois. (*Exits.*)

Enter Lord Liverpool.

George Yes. The carrot and the stick. You have persuaded me, and confirmed that my advisers were correct in urging me to support you.

Liverpool And I shall try to support you, your Majesty, but let me say that I will not be your puppet and you shall not be mine or my Government's. My earnest desire is for a nation ruled much as it is now, by those of us most fit.

George I agree. You're a good man, Lord Liverpool. We could get along famously.

Liverpool I believe that may be so, your Majesty.

George Who will inform her?

Liverpool I thought Mr Brougham, her intermediary with Parliament.

George That makes sense.

Liverpool She trusts him.

SCENE TWO

Italy.
  A joyous dance on the terrace of the Villa d'Este.
  Caroline wears a pink décolleté bodice, pink feathered head-dress, short white skirt.
  The dance leaves them all breathless. They applaud the musicians.

Dancers Bravo! Bravo!

Enter Brougham.

Brougham Excuse me. Sorry to bother you. Sorry to interrupt, but an Italian sent me out here. I think we had a language problem. I tried to tell her we are looking for –

Caroline Hello, Mr Brougham.

Brougham What? Do I know? . . . Good Heavens.

Caroline Do come and sit in the shade. You look exceedingly hot and bothered.

Brougham Erm . . . Should I return later?

Caroline Not at all. I want to know the reason for this unexpected pleasure.

Brougham The unexpectedness appears to have caught you unawares.

Caroline Oh, my dress. We have been dancing, Mr Brougham. Please, sit.

Bartolomeo Here.

Caroline This is Mr Brougham, who helped negotiate my departure from England and now administers my income from there; this is Count Bartolomeo Pergami, who administers my finances here in Italy. My Chancellor of the Exchequer, so to speak.

Brougham How do you do, sir?

Bartolomeo *Enchanté.*

Caroline And this is Billy Austin.

Brougham Good grief, is it? Hello.

Billy Hello.

Caroline Billy, do you remember Mr Brougham?

Billy Not really.

Caroline Mariette is still with me, too. She's about, somewhere. Shall you have some wine? Or water? Or coffee? Or tea? I think there is some tea.

Brougham Could I trouble you for some water, please?

Caroline It's no trouble. Billy can draw it from the well.

Enter Denman.

Denman Mr Brougham?

Brougham Ah, Denman.

Denman May I have a drink before we continue our search?

Brougham Mr Denman –

Denman Damned hot. Feel like throwing myself in the lake. These locals have the right idea, wearing next to nothing.

Brougham Mr Denman, we have found her.

Denman Eh? Oh . . . Oh gosh. Oh my . . . Oh –

Caroline It's all right, Mr Denman.

Denman Please forgive me. I'm so sorry.

Caroline As I explained to Mr Brougham, these are my dancing clothes.

Denman Your Majesty, it was my mistake –

Caroline Your Majesty?

Denman Long live the Queen!

Brougham Long live the Queen!

Caroline He died? The King has died?

Brougham Yes, your Majesty.

Caroline I thought he would go on for ever. Can we all be still and silent? Is that the correct thing to do?

Brougham If that is what your Majesty requires.

Caroline That being done. I feel I should be dressed more appropriately. Mariette?

Mariette Yes, your Majesty.

Caroline Don't call me that.

Mariette What else should I call you?

Caroline I don't know.

Exit Caroline and Mariette.

Denman That's her?

Brougham And Pergami.

Denman Do you think it's true about them?

Brougham What does it look like to you? Mr Denman, are you steadfast in our purpose?

Denman Yes, of course.

Brougham Do we care for the Prime Minister?

Denman No.

Brougham Or the party in Government?

Denman Hopeless old reactionaries.

Brougham And are we ambitious?

Denman We are.

Brougham Then let us persuade the Queen to agree to come home.

Bartolomeo Mr Brougham and Mr Denman; I hope you have the best intentions.

Brougham I don't quite catch your drift, sir.

Bartolomeo I understand someone had to be the messenger, but I wonder what happens now?

Brougham That is for the Queen to consider.

Bartolomeo You have other messages?

Brougham For the Queen, yes.

Denman You must understand, sir, that this strikes at the very heart of the British Constitution.

Brougham Our nation could descend into turmoil.

Bartolomeo And do you like that? Or do you not like that?

Brougham We don't follow you, sir.

Bartolomeo We shall see. I shall also change my dress. (*Exits.*)

Denman How do you do?

Billy Hello.

Denman Are you English?

Billy Yes.

Brougham This is William Austin.

Billy There's going to be trouble, isn't there?

Brougham Perhaps not trouble.

Billy What, then?

Brougham Negotiations.

Billy We're happy here.

Brougham And there is no reason for that to change.

Billy Where she goes, I go.

Denman Do you know where that might be?

Billy No. Do you want her to go back?

Brougham We shall advise the Queen of the decisions she is demanded to make by her position.

Exit Billy.

Denman We are going to have our work cut out.

SCENE THREE

Near the Villa.

McMahon So, Signor Majocchi. What can you tell me?

Majocchi Before I tell you what I know, please, tell me for what purpose is this information?

McMahon For the purposes of the truth.

Majocchi Yes, but I tell you, and then?

McMahon In the event it becomes necessary, any witnesses will be transported to London at no expense to themselves and compensated for any debts or losses incurred because of their journey.

Majocchi Compensation is very difficult to calculate. For instance, if I have a shop and I leave it, then who knows who might arrive in my absence to make a purchase? Maybe a large purchase, and the shop is shut. There is no way of knowing.

McMahon Any compensation shall err on the generous.

Majocchi Would the compensations be paid before or after London?

McMahon There would be some paid before, and some after the event – if there is an event. You have a shop?

Majocchi No.

McMahon Then it was, what, an example?

Majocchi A for-instance. There are others who may know something who may have shops.

McMahon What is your profession?

Majocchi I am a businessman.

McMahon Are you involved in a particular commodity?

Majocchi I trade. I buy and sell. I import/export.

McMahon I wonder if you may be looking to expand your trade? I might be able to help. But that's a separate issue. I wouldn't be doing that because of anything you've told me, I'd be doing it because I like you. We have to be very careful that there is no monetary relationship between us that could be misconstrued. I want to make sure you know what you and anyone else could be getting themselves into. Some very clever lawyers would cross-examine the witnesses.

Majocchi *Si*.

McMahon In that case, can you first tell me about Bartolomeo Pergami?

Majocchi What kind of thing?

McMahon Who is he?

Majocchi A man.

McMahon Can you be a little more forthcoming? Treat this as a rehearsal. Imagine you are in the House of Lords, surrounded by the four hundred pre-eminent men in England. I shall take on the role of a hostile lawyer. Signor Majocchi; when did you first meet Bartolomeo Pergami?

Majocchi When we were small. We grow up in the same village.

McMahon Village? Are we given to understand that Bartolomeo Pergami is a commoner?

Majocchi Commoner?

McMahon It's a term for anyone who isn't noble by birth.

Majocchi Ah, noble. Yes, he is noble. He stands very tall and broad, and in the war against –

McMahon I think you misunderstand. I'm not asking you if he behaves nobly, I'm asking if he is noble; that is, born into nobility. Titles, does he have any titles?

Majocchi He is the Baron of Augusta.

McMahon Then he is from a family of distinction?

Majocchi She buy it for him. A villa with which go the title.

McMahon Why did she do that?

Majocchi I do not know.

McMahon What could a reasonable man infer from her action?

Majocchi Is Signor Pergami in trouble?

McMahon Not if he stays out of England.

Majocchi Is anyone who goes to England in trouble?

McMahon Not if they are innocent. Before the Baron of Augusta held that title, what title, if any, did he possess?

Majocchi None.

McMahon Thank you.

Majocchi That is all? That is all I have to say?

McMahon Now we come on to what you have seen of the nature of the relationship between Signor Pergami and the Princess. Please describe what you have seen.

Majocchi Such as?

McMahon You know the sort of thing, I'm sure.

Majocchi Once I saw the Princess ride a donkey.

McMahon Is this the donkey she rode into Jerusalem?

Majocchi *Si*, Signor Pergami pick her up and put her on the ass.

McMahon You saw him pick her up?

Majocchi *Si*.

McMahon Can you demonstrate to the Lords exactly how their persons were configured?

Majocchi Like . . . So. Then so. Then so. Then this is the donkey ass. Then like so. Then like –

McMahon Thank you, Signor Majocchi. I think we have the picture.

Majocchi That is enough?

McMahon That incident is quite interesting, incriminating, even; but not important enough on its own, so unless you have anything else, I shan't trouble you further.

Majocchi Signor Pergami had been kicked by a horse and was laid up, and I was looking after him. His room was separated from hers by a small corridor with a side-room, I was sleeping in the side-room, for five or six nights.

McMahon And?

Majocchi Twice I saw the Princess pass through after midnight.

McMahon En route to where?

Majocchi The passage went only to his room.

McMahon Then what did you see?

Majocchi The door.

McMahon And what, if anything, did you hear emanate from his room when she was inside?

Majocchi Nothing. Whispers.

McMahon Whispers?

Majocchi Yes. Pss. Pss. Pss.

McMahon What do you infer from the clandestine entry of an unattended woman into a man's bedroom, at midnight?

A knock.

Is this her?

Majocchi I look.

Enter Louise Demont.

McMahon Miss Demont? You are not under any oath or any duty, Signora Demont. What you are about to tell me must be of your own free will, and, as I have explained to Signor Majocchi, if it becomes necessary, and your testimony is considered important enough, then you shall be invited to London and compensated for any difficulties that voyage may entail. But you must be clear that you are not to consider that you are paid for your testimony.

Demont I understand.

McMahon You still are in the employ of Princess Caroline?

Demont She is now Queen Caroline.

McMahon Technically, yes. But I prefer to call her the Princess of Wales for the time being. You have some information about a picture, I believe?

Demont Yes. When we were in Sicily her portrait was painted as a penitent Mary Magdalene.

McMahon Mary Magdalene, indeed? The woman of ill-repute who was saved by Jesus. What, apart from the symbolism, is significant about the portrait?

Demont The upper part is uncovered.

McMahon The upper part of what, is uncovered?

Demont Her.

McMahon She is uncovered? Her person? Her upper part?

Demont Yes.

McMahon I need to understand how far down is uncovered.

Demont To here.

McMahon Are we to be given to understand that you are saying that in this portrait, which the Princess sat for, she has her breast uncovered?

Demont Yes.

McMahon Are you really telling me that there is in existence a picture of the Princess of Wales's naked breast?

Demont Yes.

McMahon Where is this picture?

Demont It was lost in a storm at sea. He was distraught.

McMahon Who was distraught?

Demont Signor Pergami.

McMahon Why? What has this to do with him?

Demont She had commissioned the portrait as a present for him.

McMahon She gave him her portrait in which she is seen partially naked?

Demont Yes.

A knock. Enter Galdini.

McMahon And you are?

Galdini My name is Galdini. I have seen them. (*no gesture*)

SCENE FOUR

Terrace, Villa d'Este.
Caroline, Billy, Bartolomeo, Brougham, Denman.

Brougham Ma'am, there are pressing items. The passing of George III has brought to the fore many questions which, previously simmering, are now boiling. Ma'am, would it be at all possible for us to have a private audience?

Caroline This is private.

Brougham Certain parties wonder what your ambitions are now George III is dead.

Caroline What are their ambitions?

Brougham That rather depends on your ambitions.

Caroline And my ambitions rather depend on their ambitions.

Brougham Your Majesty, I have always been on your side and remain so, and it is my unpleasant duty to inform you that the King seeks to divorce you.

Caroline Divorce me?

Denman He has persuaded the Tories to allow it.

Brougham The King has persuaded the Tories to instigate a Bill of Pains and Penalties against you, Ma'am. It is not a trial as such – but it is. There is no point pretending it is not. Witnesses, cross-examination, advocacy and a verdict, and whilst the verdict is neither guilty nor not guilty, but 'content' or 'not content' that adultery has taken place, it is guilt or innocence that is being established.

Denman This Bill is activated once you set foot on English soil.

Caroline This Bill is written?

Brougham It is.

Caroline But I do not understand; if I do not return, the Bill is not activated? Then if I do not return he has no chance to divorce me. Then I shall not return.

Brougham We suggest that a failure to return would be construed as an admission of guilt.

Caroline You suggest, or you know?

Denman We strongly suggest –

Brougham It is our belief –

Denman That having taken the step of drawing the Bill, the King and his Government are unlikely to retract or discard it even should you not return.

Brougham They will use it whenever they deem it expedient.

Caroline Then it hangs over me. Return and risk being found guilty; stay and be construed guilty?

Brougham But we may assure you that as a woman, this Bill is not an attempt to make you liable to penal justice, as a woman you are only an accessory to adultery.

Denman The man, however, would be guilty of treason.

Caroline Who is named as my adulterer?

Denman We are afraid it is this gentleman, Signor Pergami.

Caroline That Bill is a lie. I have never been intimate with any man except my husband.

Brougham Of course not, Ma'am.

Bartolomeo *Excusi.* (*Exits.*)

Caroline What is the burden of proof required to pass the Bill?

Brougham *In flagrante delicto*, or at least overwhelming circumstance.

Caroline I can assure you that *in flagrante* is not a possibility.

Brougham Of course not, Ma'am, but as to circumstantial evidence, they have spies watching you all the time; innocent relationships may be wilfully misconstrued.

Caroline Baron Pergami – he is accused of treason?

Denman He cannot be tried for treason if he stays out of England.

Caroline Do I have any other supporters?

Billy – I don't think you should go back –

Denman – Many.

Caroline Billy, find Baron Pergami and bring him here, please.

Exit Billy.

Brougham In allying himself to the Tories the King has positioned himself against reforms. Those committed to reform are prepared to rally around you.

Denman In the country the people –

Brougham Excluded from government –

Denman Support you.

Brougham Cry out for you.

Enter Demont.

Demont Excuse me, Ma'am, but may I speak with you?

Caroline Not now, Louise.

Demont Ma'am, it is urgent that I speak –

Caroline Louise, fetch brandy, please.

Demont Ma'am, I have some inform –

Caroline Not now! Brandy!

Exit Demont.

Denman The King and the Tories are terrified you might return because the nation is split between you and him.

Brougham The King has already ordered your name be removed from prayers.

Caroline Removed?

Brougham You are not to be mentioned.

Denman The situation is volatile.

Brougham So volatile that the government is prepared to offer you £50,000 a year to stay away.

Denman But how can you trust them?

Caroline Does the King seek to re-marry?

Brougham It is true that since the tragic deaths of your daughter and grandson he has no direct heir.

Caroline I pray every day for my daughter and her still-born son.

Brougham It was most unfortunate. The nation was much affected.

Caroline I wasn't informed of the tragedy.

Brougham You weren't what?

Caroline I wasn't told of their deaths.

Brougham Your Majesty, if I had been aware that you hadn't been told –

Caroline A man, a traveller passing by; he told me. Could you excuse me for a while? Ask Louise to look after you. She's in the house fetching my brandy.

Brougham Ma'am, I assure you that we are convinced yours is the just cause.

Exit Brougham and Denman.
Enter Mariette.

Caroline Where's Louise with my brandy?

Mariette I did not see her, Ma'am, I'm about to prepare your dress for the morning, and I need your instructions as to what it might be.

Caroline I do not yet know.

Mariette Ma'am, I am wondering if I should break out the more formal attire.

Caroline I do not yet know.

Mariette Ma'am, I am wondering if you are to be dressing as you have been this last while, or regally?

Caroline I shall inform you what I have decided, when I have decided.

Mariette Ma'am, you are Queen of England, so your dress and behaviour should reflect that heritage.

Caroline Wasn't it you who encouraged me to defy my husband?

Enter Billy and Bartolomeo.

Mariette At the time, Ma'am, I could not foresee how far that defiance would lead you from your duty.

Caroline Mariette, he tries to divorce me.

Mariette I never thought it would go so far. Plead his forgiveness.

Bartolomeo No! She does not plead to anyone!

Mariette You don't understand.

Bartolomeo No, you do not understand.

Mariette She is the Queen of England; do you think you may advise her now? Would you be what, her Prime Minister? And would William Austin be what – Admiral of the Fleet? No, because you are an Italian commoner, and his mother is a washerwoman.

Billy My mother is a laundress!

Mariette Washerwoman, laundress; the same.

Billy My mother is the best laundress in Deptford!

Mariette And she abandoned you and her Majesty has elevated you to beyond what your mother could have

81

dreamed. And now you and he are terrified that your benefactress has cares more pressing than her provision of your comfort.

Bartolomeo All these years you have been waiting –

Mariette We all have.

Caroline Mariette, I shall talk to you later.

Mariette I await your instructions. (*Exits.*)

Caroline Tell Louise to bring my brandy!

Billy There will be trouble if you go back.

Caroline Billy, could we be alone for a while, please?

Billy Where you go, I go. (*Exits.*)

Bartolomeo Those two Englishmen are not your friends.

Caroline They are not required to be. I immediately have numerous appointments in my gift. I shall make Mr Brougham my Attorney General and Mr Denman my Solicitor General.

Bartolomeo You serve their ends.

Caroline And they, mine.

Bartolomeo The way George attacks, the way you retaliate; you hate each other as if you are lovers.

Caroline I have to fight him –

Bartolomeo Love and hate are not opposites; they share the same opposite – indifference is the opposite to both love and hate. Can you not be indifferent to him?

Caroline He married me in bad faith, he humiliated me, he divided me from my child, excluded me from her death, and now he seeks to disgrace and disinherit me. Can you let him persecute me without allowing me to defend myself? I cannot let him prosper, I could not live in peace knowing he had won and I did not fight.

Bartolomeo If you have to return, then I shall go with you.

Caroline You cannot. Once you are in England, if adultery is found, you would be guilty of treason.

Bartolomeo But I would not have abandoned you.

Caroline Please; it will comfort me to know that you are here. In order to beat off this Bill I shall have to deny you.

Bartolomeo I know that, you have done it once already, I am sorry I had to walk away –

Caroline Bartolomeo, people look at us and they know.

Bartolomeo I shall be more in control, I will compose my features like an Englishman, take on an English disposition, give nothing away –

Caroline No. I am trained for that, you are not. I shall go, resolve this, and then I shall return to you for ever.

Bartolomeo You swear to return?

Caroline He must be thwarted –

Bartolomeo Please, please, just do the smallest things, do not provoke him into vengeful –

Caroline It is he who is vengeful.

Bartolomeo In Italy we call this a vendetta.

Caroline I shall only do what is necessary.

Bartolomeo That is exactly the kind of thing said by persons engaged in a vendetta. Please, yes, I beg you, keep your judgement. I see the flash in your eyes. You shall be there whilst I am here. Please, keep safe. And what shall I do whilst you are away? Already I feel sick to my stomach –

Caroline Bartolomeo; please wait for me.

Bartolomeo Yes. Yes, of course. How long shall it be?

Caroline Less than a year.

Bartolomeo Less than a year. Then that means up to a year. I shall weep.

Caroline More than now?

Bartolomeo More.

Caroline I shall write to you, and have the letters sent. I shall have to write in code.

Bartolomeo You are my Queen. You have always been my Queen. You are my sovereign, and I am your nation, your land, and your people. I am your army and your navy, and your adoring public.

Caroline May we have a dance alone?

Bartolomeo Here? With no music?

Caroline We can imagine the music.

A slow dance.

Bartolomeo In the morning, when we bid farewell, we cannot be as we are now, can we?

Caroline No. Keep dancing.

Act Three

SCENE ONE

London. A palace.

McMahon She's landed at Dover. There are crowds. The garrison fired a salute because they did not know what else to do. No one knows whether to pay tribute or not.

George Should I forbid it?

McMahon No, because then if they still saluted her you would have to do something about it. Better the confusion.

George How does she appear?

McMahon The people unhitched the horses and drew her carriage themselves. (*Exits.*)

Enter Prince William, Lord Liverpool and Lord Malmesbury.

George Lords. William.

Liverpool and Malmesbury Majesty.

William George.

Liverpool Your Majesty, conscious as we are that the arrival in the capital of the defendant named in the Bill of Pains and Penalties is imminent, we feel compelled to approach your Majesty that we might urge you to reconsider the course of action her return occasions.

George Go on, Prime Minister.

William The thing is, George. Now it's come to it; now she seems to have picked up the gauntlet, some are wavering.

Liverpool As your Government, your Majesty, we must be mindful of the mood of the nation.

George But the Bill is drawn – and its existence widely known. If we withdraw now because she returns then we appear afraid of her.

Liverpool Our consciences demand that we urgently consider the safety of the people.

George How odd? I've found a politician's conscience usually demands only the urgent considering of his own interest.

William The politicians protest they have no interest as such in this matter, except that they fear that she shall become a rallying point for dissenters.

George She is already that. She is being defended by the man you commissioned to enact your plan, and she is being courted and supported by the radical element in the Whig party and the extremists who lurk in the shadows behind them. So if you are prepared to risk the end of everything we know and hold dear and cherish, then yes, convince me I should let her off, sit with her, smile as she is crowned; then see what she does. And when she has done it, and everything lies in ruins around us, I promise I shall not say 'I told you so.'

Liverpool Yes, but even after the Bill there will still be strong objection to divorce.

George Then divorce must be weighed against adultery. If she was your wife what would you do? If she was your wife and she went to Italy and had sexual intercourse with a peasant what would you do? Lord Malmesbury?

Malmesbury I think, given all that has gone before, we have no choice.

George Meaning?

Malmesbury Why return if she is not innocent? Or, at least, believes herself more sinned against than sinning. Your Majesty. (*Exits.*)

Liverpool Your Majesty, I understand Lord Malmesbury is deeply grieving the death of your father, and as you know, grief can temporarily affect one's judgment.

George Thank you, Prime Minister.

Liverpool I am sorry for what Mr Brougham has done, but not as sorry as he shall be.

Exit Lord Liverpool.

William Well argued, George. (*Exits.*)

Enter McMahon.

McMahon They waver?

George Yes. But they will proceed.

McMahon She is en route to Canterbury with a growing entourage including Messrs Brougham and Denman – against both of whom we can find nothing. They shall stay at a house in Mayfair.

George How popular is she?

McMahon It's hard to tell, sir. It might just be the novelty of her. It could wear off. I don't think mobs really think these things through.

SCENE TWO

The upstairs of a house in Mayfair.
  Off, a crowd.

Crowd God save the Queen.

Denman She's an odd woman to be Queen.

Brougham Rather frank in her expressions.

Denman But she has been living with ordinary people.

Brougham She looks the part, and is gracious to the
crowds, who seem to love her.

Denman Listen to them.

Brougham Any news of their Italian witnesses?

Denman Beyond the fact they've arrived, no.

Brougham Keep at it. If she can maintain her decorum,
then all we have to worry about is destroying the evidence.
We'll give her the best defence a man can, won't we,
Denman?

Denman The very, very best. But what if we lose?

  Enter Caroline, Billy and Mariette.

Caroline I don't see how that can occur, Mr Denman,
when I am being defended by the best advocates in
England and I am innocent. And the English people, they
are calling for me.

Brougham (*a list*) And these persons are calling on you.

Caroline I shall receive her.

Brougham Really?

Caroline Yes, really. Shall I go out?

  She goes out on the balcony. The crowd cheers.

Crowd The Queen, the Queen for ever!

Caroline I want no mobs. This crowd must not become a mob.

Brougham You cannot be held responsible for the behaviour of the masses.

Caroline These people are here because I am.

Enter Lady Jersey.

Lady Jersey Your Majesty.

Caroline Lady Jersey. I am absolutely delighted to see you.

Lady Jersey Your Majesty is too kind.

Caroline Lady Jersey, these are my friends and protectors: Mr Brougham and Mr Denman. Are you acquainted?

Lady Jersey Only with their reputations.

Caroline I expect they have heard of you also. Would the gentlemen mind leaving us for a while? I'm sure you have some weighty legal matters to discuss.

Brougham We'd be quite happy to remain here.

Caroline I think I have had enough serious talk. I need some female company.

Exit Brougham and Denman.

Billy, could you pass me paper and pen? Excuse me for a moment, Lady Jersey. An urgent note. Here, Billy, take that for me would you?

Billy Ma'am.

Exit Billy.

Lady Jersey Is that really William Austin?

Caroline Indeed it is. And do you remember Mariette?

Lady Jersey Yes, of course.

Mariette Lady Jersey.

Caroline Mariette, I shan't need anything for a while.

Mariette Ma'am. (*Exits.*)

Caroline I'm so pleased you called.

Lady Jersey I'm grateful that you noticed my name on the list.

Caroline You are one of the people I had it in mind to see soonest. Are you unpopular with either of those gentlemen?

Lady Jersey Not for any reason I am conscious of.

Caroline Then they are scared of you. And me.

Lady Jersey Your return has aroused a great deal of agitation.

Caroline I have no desire to harm anyone.

Lady Jersey You do look very well. Italy obviously suits you.

Caroline It did. The years haven't changed you.

Lady Jersey My unguents and potions. And you've dyed your hair.

Caroline How is Lord Jersey?

Lady Jersey Very well. We fell out quite seriously for a while until we realised we couldn't quite manage without each other. It was only a disagreement about money. He was being threatened with debtors' prison.

Caroline I thought persons who had held the positions you had received pensions?

Lady Jersey There was mention.

Caroline Have you never received a pension from the crown?

Lady Jersey No.

Caroline I shall attend to that after my Coronation. How is George?

Lady Jersey I haven't seen him.

Caroline Since when?

Lady Jersey I remember you now; you are the woman who asks me direct questions. I haven't seen him since the twelfth of June, 1817, and that was at a distance. I was on London Bridge in a carriage when he passed underneath in his barge. I saw that he saw me but he did not acknowledge me. He's scared of you.

Caroline Is that fact, or speculation?

Lady Jersey He's petrified that you may be more popular than he. The people are already dividing into 'Kingites' and 'Queenites', terms synonymous with Tory and Whig.

Caroline And the Radicals are with the Whigs?

Lady Jersey In this, yes.

Caroline What about the Revolutionaries?

Lady Jersey I haven't any to call upon to ask but I am led to understand that you have also become their rallying point, for want of any other.

Caroline One can hardly be a revolutionary Queen.

Lady Jersey Indeed, if they helped you to power they would then immediately have to attempt a revolution to overthrow you.

Caroline Am I coming to power? I thought I was on trial.

Lady Jersey You enjoy an immense amount of goodwill founded on a keen sense of injustice. I think if you had been crowned with no fuss or bother or comment it could have been bluffed out. But this way, the people know they can't settle until it's over.

Caroline Is there a real risk of civil conflict?

Lady Jersey Rumours have always abounded that you would return when the King died. And then landing at Dover, proceeding to Canterbury – these places are symbolic.

Caroline It's been rather more auspicious than my first arrival.

Lady Jersey Shall you go to the Lords? All those men discussing your intimate relations.

Caroline There aren't any intimate relations for them to discuss.

Lady Jersey No. Of course not.

Caroline How is Mrs Fitzherbert?

Lady Jersey Reports say she is well.

Caroline What would happen if the Government and the King were directly confronted about her?

Lady Jersey More anti-Catholic riots, I expect. You must be acquainted with many Catholics in Italy.

Caroline Frances; can you do something for me?

Lady Jersey What?

Caroline There's hardly anyone I can trust.

Lady Jersey I expect so many people try to take advantage.

Caroline Human nature.

Lady Jersey You top the ivory tower. We may climb up to be near you, but we find that the last stretch has no footholds, so all we may do is crane our necks, squint into the sun, and hang on for as long as we can.

Caroline Can you take a message to George for me? Can you tell him I would like to speak sympathetically with him?

Lady Jersey I'm afraid I am unable to do that.

Caroline That is all you have to convey.

Lady Jersey Apart from some fainthearts, everyone, myself included, wants to see what shall happen. All the people out there, all your gentlemen protectors, all the husbands, the wives, the stupid and the kind, we all want to see how this conflict is reconciled. I'm fascinated. I don't wish you any harm, but I'm fascinated to see. You can't stop this now. If you could bind any Briton to reply truthfully to the question: 'Do you wish to hear the intimate details of the Queen's relationship with a tall, dark, handsome Italian?' – all, all would have to answer 'Yes.' The papers are full of you. There are toys, souvenirs, ballads. One woman may not possess the courage to endure that which awaits you – if ever you feel your courage failing, please send for me – but no, I won't carry a message to George. Don't trust me. I tried being at the centre of things and I was wounded. Now I'm satisfied to be at the perimeter, watching. (*Exits.*)

Caroline You may go now.

Enter Billy.

Safely delivered?

Billy He asked for more money. He says the last courier was nearly caught at the coast.

Caroline I shall give you some.

*Exit Billy. A pain in Caroline's abdomen. She
recovers. She goes out again onto the balcony and the
crowd erupts.*

SCENE THREE

*Co-existing: streets, apartments, the House of Lords.
Noise.*

i

Lord Chancellor (Speaker) Order! Order! The Prime
Minister.

Liverpool In the year one thousand eight hundred and
fourteen, Caroline Amelia Elizabeth, then Princess of
Wales, and now Queen Consort of this realm, at Milan,
in Italy, engaged in her service, in a menial situation, one
Bartolomeo Pergami, a foreigner of low station, and a
most unbecoming and degrading intimacy commenced
between her Royal Highness and the said Bartolomeo
Pergami, and further unmindful of her exalted rank and
station, or of her duty to the King, and wholly regardless
of her own honour and character, she conducted herself
towards the said Bartolomeo Pergami, both in public and
in private, with indecent familiarity and freedom, and
carried on a licentious, disgraceful, and adulterous intercourse, by which conduct of her said Royal Highness,
great scandal and dishonour have been brought upon his
Majesty's family and this kingdom. And be it enacted in
this present Parliament assembled, her said Majesty
Caroline Amelia Elizabeth, from and after the passing of
this Act, shall be and is hereafter deprived of the title of
Queen, and of all the prerogatives, rights, privileges, and
exemptions appertaining thereto; and moreover, if this

Bill is passed, the marriage between his Majesty and the said Caroline Amelia Elizabeth be for ever dissolved, annulled, and made void to all intents, constructions, and purposes whatsoever.

ii

Gifford Signor Majocchi, as well as your evidence regarding the visits paid to Pergami's bedchamber by the Princess, you witnessed a certain display in Jaffa, did you not?

Majocchi Yes, sir.

Gifford Would you be so kind as to tell the Lords what this display was?

Majocchi It was a dance by Mahomet the Exhibitionist.

Gifford Were the Princess and Pergami present?

Majocchi Yes.

Gifford Can you describe the performance of this Mahomet the Exhibitionist?

Majocchi He performed a *giuco*.

Gifford A *giuco* is a dance?

Majocchi *Si*.

Gifford Could you describe it?

Majocchi It . . . Er . . . He . . . You . . .

Gifford Was anything done by Mahomet with any part of his dress?

Majocchi He made use of the linen of his large pantaloons.

Gifford Can you describe what use he made of the linen in the pantaloons?

Majocchi He made the pantaloons . . . How do you say? Like this.

Gifford Thank you, Signor Majocchi. As you can see, gentlemen. Mahomet the Exhibitionist made the material of his pantaloons move backwards and forwards.

iii

Caroline (*pain, laudanum*) Bartolomeo; Majocchi is giving evidence. One of your friends is here.

iv

Brougham (*Denman is with him*) At one time you were employed by the Princess at her house, were you not?

Majocchi Yes.

Brougham Why did you leave?

Majocchi She tell me to go.

Brougham Why was that?

Majocchi Some items were missing and she blamed me.

Brougham What items?

Majocchi From the kitchen.

Brougham But you have no knowledge of these missing items?

Majocchi No. And there was no proof.

Brougham And do you feel vengeful towards her?

Majocchi No.

Brougham Then why are you here?

Gifford He's been called as a witness.

Majocchi *Si.* Yes.

Brougham Signor Majocchi; where are you staying in London?

Majocchi At a hotel.

Brougham An expensive hotel?

Majocchi No.

Brougham An inexpensive hotel?

Majocchi No. I do not know.

Brougham You do not know the price of your hotel?

Majocchi I do not pay.

Gifford He was called as a witness, he doesn't have to pay.

Brougham Signor Majocchi; when you slept off the corridor between the Princess's and Pergami's bedchambers, what divided your chamber from the corridor?

Majocchi A curtain.

Brougham And was the curtain open or closed?

Majocchi Open.

Brougham And you are sure there was no other way from the Princess's room to Pergami's?

Majocchi I speak of one passage. I have only seen that one that I remember.

Brougham Only one that you remember?

Majocchi *Si.*

Brougham Only one that you remember?

Majocchi *Si.*

Brougham Do you swear that there was no other way from the Princess's room to Pergami's room? If you are in any doubt, any doubt at all –

Majocchi *Non mi ricordo.*

Brougham Does that mean 'I don't recollect' or 'I don't know'?

Majocchi *Non mi ricordo.*

Brougham If I wanted to say 'I don't know', I would say '*no so*'. If I wanted to say 'I don't remember' I would say '*no mi ricordo questo*'.

Liverpool (*aside*) I didn't know Brougham could speak Italian languages.

Gifford (*aside*) Neither did I.

Brougham So if I ask you again to swear that there was no other way from the Princess's room to Pergami's room?

Majocchi *Non mi ricordo.*

Brougham You don't remember. Is it not strange, that if there might be another way between the Princess's bedroom and Pergami's, that she would choose to journey along the one where you slept, if she were concerned to keep her journey secret? Do you remember how the Princess was dressed when she passed en route to Pergami's bedroom?

Majocchi *Non mi ricordo.*

Liverpool (*aside*) The Italian's stuck.

Gifford (*aside*) He's terrified.

Brougham Did you see her Royal Highness distinctly on that occasion?

Liverpool (*aside*) Say yes!

Majocchi Yes.

Brougham But you do not remember how she was dressed?

Majocchi I do not remember what dress she had.

William (*aside*) Then bloody make one up!

v

Caroline Mr Brougham sent Majocchi's head spinning. He answered '*Non mi ricordo*' eighty-seven times! How is the lake?

vi

McMahon The seed is sown. The inference is enough. Brougham broke the witness but didn't discredit his story.

George What about these caricatures of me?

McMahon Regrettable, but not serious.

George Pay them off. Pay them not to print.

McMahon If you let it be known, sir, that you shall pay men not to print caricatures of you, ten million Englishmen shall immediately confess to have been about to undertake that very enterprise and claim their reward.

George Then what do you advise?

McMahon We keep a list, sir, then when this is over we remember who your friends were.

George What is she doing?

McMahon She listens, and watches. Between sessions she plays backgammon in an ante-room. And I think that she daily sends messages; and I think I know to whom they are carried. A love letter would be as useful as an eye witness.

vii

A gang of men stops a man.

Gang The King or the Queen?

Man Both. Neither.

Gang Which?

Man The King.

Gang Wrong!

The gang beat and chase him.

viii

Gifford And this night as you went about your duties in the dressing room adjoining the Princess's bedchamber, where was the Princess?

Demont At her toilet.

Gifford And what happened?

Demont The door from the passage opened and Signor Pergami entered.

Gifford Without ceremony? What was the state of his dress?

Demont He was not dressed.

Gifford What had he on?

Demont He was not dressed at all.

Gifford At all?

Demont He had a shirt.

Gifford Had he on anything more than his shirt?

Demont His slippers.

Gifford What did you do when you saw him?

Demont I escaped.

Gifford Thank you, Miss Demont.

Brougham Signora Demont; what did you think was the purpose of Pergami's entrance?

Demont I do not know.

Brougham What did you infer?

Demont That he thought she was alone.

Brougham But you say you escaped, that is, you did not see what happened next?

Demont No.

Brougham How then can you be sure that there wasn't some proper reason for Pergami's visit? Perhaps he'd heard a noise. Perhaps he had even heard you, and directly taken action to ensure the Princess was safe.

Demont He had no pistol or sword.

Brougham Are you sure?

Enter Denman with a note for Brougham.

Demont He did not enter as if he suspected there might be an intruder.

Brougham Very well. But you did not see what transpired, because you 'escaped' as you put it.

Demont Yes.

Brougham Since leaving the employ of her Royal Highness you have lived in London, I understand?

Demont I have.

Brougham Have you always been known as Louise Demont?

Liverpool (*aside*) What's this?

Gifford (*aside*) I don't know.

Demont Yes, I have.

Liverpool (*aside*) He's shaken her.

Brougham Are you sure that no one in London knows you by any other name? Do you know the name Colombier?

Demont In London I have sometimes taken the name of the place I was born.

Brougham That is Colombier?

Liverpool (*aside*) Gifford?

Gifford (*aside*) I didn't know this.

Demont Yes.

Brougham Louise Colombier, or Countess Colombier?

Demont Louise.

Brougham Are you aware that a lady calling herself Countess Colombier has been going about London running up debts in respect of haberdashery, millinery, servants and dining out?

Demont No.

Brougham You never called yourself a Countess?

Liverpool (*aside*) Just tell him no.

Demont I do not swear it, but I do not recollect it.

Brougham Would your answer therefore be '*non mi ricordo*', by any chance? And now let us turn to this portrait you say you saw.

ix

Caroline Poor thing. Tied in knots. Take this. (*She hands a letter to Billy.*)

x

Billy is intercepted by McMahon and a gang of men.

McMahon Kingite or Queenite?

Billy Queenite to the death!

McMahon That could be arranged.

   The gang beat Billy. McMahon finds the letter.

The guards are coming!

   The gang runs off.

What's this?

Billy I don't know.

McMahon No address? Who is it for?

Billy I don't know!

McMahon It's about food.

Billy Is it?

McMahon Is it a code? What does it mean?

Billy 'Last night I dreamt of a capon, *stuffed* with a hare, *stuffed* with figs, all *stuffed* to bursting . . . Heavenly' –

Billy laughs. McMahon strikes him.

xi

George Is it proven, yet?

William I think it is.

George You think it is?

William Not proven, but obvious.

xii

Caroline Billy was beaten.

Brougham I'm sorry to hear that.

Caroline Mobs and gangs. I don't want anyone hurt.

Brougham It's a dirty fight, Ma'am.

Caroline But my defence must be dignified. And I do not like these sentiments against the Italians.

Brougham We haven't consciously cultivated it, Ma'am.

Caroline And neither should you exploit it.

Brougham Ma'am.

xiii

Malmesbury This is the most degrading, disgraceful display I have ever witnessed. Even if adultery is proved I and many others may protest by voting against the Bill.

Liverpool I think we should remain resolute.

Malmesbury We expose ourselves to ridicule.

Liverpool If we don't find her guilty we do.

Malmesbury How can our party be seen to favour divorce?

Liverpool You brought her to this country, didn't you?

Malmesbury I have done nothing to be ashamed of. I am not her husband.

Liverpool What about her? Do you think she's ashamed?

xiv

George What's this about mobs?

McMahon *The Rights of Man* is being openly sold on the streets.

George Anyone hurt?

McMahon Five dead, sir. Looters.

George What about more witnesses for us?

McMahon There are rumours in Italy that Kingite witnesses are being beaten and even killed by Queenite Englishmen.

George We'll give them armed escort.

McMahon I have to say, sir, Mr Brougham is brilliant. You should think of him for a senior position.

George Perhaps he should know that I'm thinking that. And Mrs Fitzherbert, is she well?

McMahon I am assured she is, sir.

Gifford So when the Princess's party sailed to the Holy Land the Princess slept in a tent on deck, two tents, in fact, one inside the other?

Galdini Yes.

Gifford Did anybody sleep under the same tent?

Galdini Bartolomeo Pergami.

Gifford Were the sides of the tent drawn in, so as to shut them entirely in?

Galdini When they went to sleep the whole was enclosed, shut up.

Gifford And where did you sleep?

Galdini Immediately below the deck where the tent was placed.

Gifford Did you ever hear any motion over you?

Galdini I have heard a noise.

Gifford What did it appear to you to be?

Galdini The creaking of a bench.

Gifford I see. Apart from what you heard, are you in possession of any other information which may help us?

Galdini Once, when I was passing, I saw the Princess and Pergami sitting together on a bench, he with his arm around her neck.

Gifford How was the Princess dressed to her bosom?

Galdini She was uncovered . . . like so.

Gifford Were they aware you saw them?

Galdini Pergami got up and told me, 'What do you want from her, you son of a bitch?'

Gifford I understand that you are only repeating what was said to you, but could you exercise slightly more restraint, please? This is the English House of Lords, and these are solemn matters.

Galdini My apologies.

Gifford Thank you.

Brougham Signor Galdini.

Liverpool (*aside*) Hold firm.

Brougham Everything creaks on a ship at sea, does it not?

Galdini This was a different kind of creaking.

Brougham Does more or less everything on a ship at sea, creak? Yes or no.

Galdini Yes.

Brougham Thank you. Now. Who else slept below decks?

Galdini Everyone else.

Brougham Everyone else apart from whom?

Galdini The Princess and Pergami.

Brougham And what were conditions like?

Galdini The usual.

Brougham Hot?

Galdini Yes.

Brougham Cramped?

Galdini Yes.

Brougham The animals were down there?

Galdini Yes.

Brougham And they were kept down there all the time?

Galdini Yes.

Brougham Could one below decks remove oneself from the odour and sound of the animals and crew?

Galdini No.

Brougham So there is discomfort involved in sleeping below decks?

Galdini Yes.

Brougham And if you had the choice of sleeping below decks, or in a tent on deck, which would you have taken?

Galdini The tent, of course –

Brougham Thank you. So on that ship at that time in that place in those circumstances, the tent on the deck were the most fitting quarters for the most prestigious passenger? Now. Two tents, one inside the other and guarded by?

Galdini Pergami.

Brougham And if you were he, where would you place yourself at night in order to defend her?

Galdini By the tent, not in the tent.

Gifford (*aside*) Good man.

Brougham You wish he had been by the tent rather than inside the outer tent, don't you?

Liverpool (*aside*) What's this?

Galdini *Excusi?*

Brougham If Pergami had taken up sentry duty outside the tents, you would have been able to see him, would you not?

Galdini See him?

Brougham See him and avoid him. Shall I tell the Lords why you wished you had seen him? Because he saw you, didn't he? He was on sentry duty in the corridor between the two tents, was he not, when you crept up to the outer tent and cut a slit in it with your knife, and next you were intending to cut a slit in the inner tent and then what did you intend?

Galdini No, no, the tent blew open and –

Brougham Pergami heard and/or saw you and gave you a hiding, did he not?

Galdini No, he kick me after I see them and he see me and –

Brougham He did his job, didn't he? Pergami punished you because he caught you engaged in an attempted assault on the future Queen of England!

Galdini I saw it, and made my escape, it was uncovered as far as here –

Brougham You didn't see anything, did you? Her guard caught you before –

Galdini I saw the breasts! I saw the breasts!

Brougham You stand in the most august chamber in the principle nation in the world and boast that you have spied on the Queen's bosom? Mister Galdini, you are the lowest specimen of humanity I have ever encountered.

Caroline Bartolomeo; they have had that Galdini here.
Mr Brougham saved me this time!

McMahon Mr Brougham?

Brougham Yes?

McMahon I represent a certain party.

Brougham As there are only two parties at present, you
must be from the enemy.

McMahon There is only one party: England. May I ask
what you expect to do after the Bill?

Brougham Continue practising the law.

McMahon As the Queen's Attorney General?

Brougham Unless she informs me otherwise.

McMahon I wonder where she shall reside, afterwards?

Brougham In St James' Palace, I hope.

McMahon Is it not possible she may reside elsewhere?

Brougham Who are you, sir?

McMahon Do you think you can make any more capital
arguing her cause?

Brougham The Government's majority shrinks every day.
More Lords stay away from the House. The people can
tell who is right and who is wrong in –

McMahon The mob is on the streets rioting and looting.
Radicals, artisans, mechanics and hooligans whipped up
in a hopeless cause.

Brougham Sir, my job is to disprove the Bill, I am not responsible for the masses.

McMahon You know she's guilty, don't you? You're a Radical yourself, are you not? You don't really want a Queen at all. You would rather a Republic. You want these riots. A Republican who makes his name hitched to the skirts of royalty.

Brougham And you, sir. What is the purpose of your existence?

McMahon Unlike yourself, I have nothing so exalted as a purpose.

Brougham Do not denigrate yourself. Even a messenger boy has purpose. Excuse me. (*Exits.*)

McMahon The witnesses have said what they saw. Everyone knows it's the truth. It's just an excuse for the mobs to play a little havoc. She won't stay. She'll return to her Italian. Why should she stay here?

Enter a gang of men.

Gang Kingite or Queenite? . . . You, Kingite or Queenite?

McMahon *Non mi ricordo.*

Gang What's that?

McMahon *Excusi?*

Gang Are you Italian?

McMahon *Si.*

The men attack him. McMahon defeats them by martial arts. The men flee in disarray.

Brougham There is a matter I would like to broach with you. Some items I seek your permission to have in reserve for my summing up should Mr Gifford's summing up go hard against us.

Caroline What items?

Brougham Your Majesty. I do not think they have done enough to pass the Bill, but I am wary that Mr Gifford still might compellingly marshall their witnesses' testimonies.

Caroline If you were Mr Gifford, could you persuade the Lords to pass the Bill?

Brougham I'd like to think that I could.

Caroline Mr Gifford does not possess your abilities. What items?

Brougham The nationality of the witnesses has most definitely become an issue. I do not seek your permission to exploit this, but I may have to mention it.

Caroline Be very careful.

Brougham Also, I need to know what you intend afterwards, in order that I might gauge the weight of my arguments – I do not want to go too far and endanger any future negotiations.

Caroline Let us defeat the Bill, then decide what happens next.

xix

Denman What was that about?

Brougham What was what about?

Denman What she intends afterwards?

Brougham To be Queen, of course.

Denman Then why were you asking?

Brougham For the reason I stated. We must not only win, but win well.

xx

Caroline (*pain, laudanum*) Bartolomeo, it's the end of the witnesses. Only the summing up. Pray for us.

xxi

Gifford All I ask from your Lordships is that you place yourselves in a plain man's shoes, and you ask yourselves, 'What would a plain man infer from what we have heard?' What would a plain man infer from the sighting, at night, of the Princess on her way to Pergami's bedchamber? What would a plain man infer from the detail of the portrait the Princess presented to Pergami which was then lost at sea? What would a plain man infer from the sighting of Pergami entering the Princess's bedchamber in a state of undress? And what of the tent on the ship, why could there not be several guards? Mr Brougham has not contested any detail of the Government's witnesses' statements. What he has done, and done very cleverly, is to ask us to regard the evidence from a different angle; to arrive at conclusions at variance from the obvious. He has attempted to beguile a plain man into thinking things are not what they obviously are. He has diverted us from the truth by attempting to destroy the credibility of our witnesses, but their testimonies stand. If any woman, any wife, had done what we have heard, it would be shocking, and disgraceful, and shameful, and an offence to public decency – all these things and more; but when that woman, that wife, is also the potential Queen of England, what example is she? Would the father of a family propose her as an example to his daughters? Should you, as fathers of the nation, propose her as an example to those who look to you for guidance? I ask you to agree with me that it is a matter of the utmost urgency that this Bill is passed; then yourselves and the nation may return your attention to more glorious, noble, and elevating considerations.

Brougham Nothing has been proven. The witnesses were paid to testify. The good name of England has been dragged through the mud. I know it. You know it. The people know it. There have been some disgraceful scenes. Italians attacked, even suspected Italians attacked. I have no sympathy for any sentiments against Italy and Italians. But I understand how these sentiments can be held, for has not Italy been the setting of choice of some of our most revered story-tellers – Shakespeare, Jonson, Webster – who knew how widely it is held that it is in Italy that cunning and artifice thrive, in Italy that a price is openly set upon an oath, in Italy that every infamous purpose might by bribery be carried into effect? One of our great story-tellers might have said 'A poisoned stiletto has been planted in the bosom of our Queen but some of us are wilfully mistaking it for a sword of justice!' All through this trial – and trial it is, for if you say you are 'content' then you are saying 'guilty' – I have struggled with the notion that you have brought this Bill unwillingly. I hope I am right in thinking there are far greater issues to which you wish you could have been applying your talents. Did you want this Bill? Did you want to hear the lies, the calumnies, the perversions? Would any of you allow your wives to be as persecuted as the Queen is? Justice. Plain man's justice. Yes. Let that guide you.

George The first reading?

Liverpool One hundred and twenty-three for, ninety-five against.

George Ninety-five men truly disbelieve her adultery?

Liverpool No, sir. The most widely held view is that one may reasonably believe in her misconduct, but there is an almost universal feeling in the House and abroad against the manner in which the House has been used, so the Lords have protested – or given in to public opinion, whichever way you choose to look at it – by voting adultery not proven. And, regardless of right and wrong, guilt or innocence, given our small majority at the first reading it is improbable that the Bill will be passed in the Commons, so my reluctant advice is that we wait until after the second reading in the Lords, then drop it.

George Then she shall have won?

Gifford No, sir –

George Shut up, Gifford.

Liverpool We shall still win the count on the second reading in the Lords, so no, your Majesty, she shall not have won.

George Bring the Bill then drop it? Of course she has won.

Liverpool A pyrrhic victory.

George You lost this Bill, Gifford – shut up, Gifford. And you presented her with her brilliant advocate.

Liverpool That is unfair, your Highness.

George She commits adultery yet I can't divorce her and you wish to discuss fairness?

Canterbury Perhaps we should return when you are more composed.

George And you – when conducting the miserable service which shackles me to this monster, you stopped on 'any person knowing of a lawful impediment' – you said it twice, in fact. How dare you!

Exit Canterbury, Liverpool, Gifford. Enter McMahon.

McMahon Sir?

George Dropped! The Bill is dropped! Everyone fails me! (*Exits.*)

McMahon Sir, I –

xxiii

Caroline Bartolomeo, we have won! Listen! Fireworks! You shall be the lover of the Queen of England!

Enter Billy.

Billy Can we go home, now?

Caroline Don't tell Mariette, but yes, after the Coronation. You want to be at my Coronation, don't you? I'll be crowned then we'll go.

Enter Brougham and Denman. Champagne.

SCENE FOUR

A palace.
George looks out at the fireworks.

Maria Come away.

George They can't see me.

Maria You're going to have to appear to be making a go of it, aren't you?

Silence.

George I'm sorry; what was that?

Maria What was what?

George I thought you said something.

Maria Her presence fills the air. I saw daubed on a wall in Drury Lane: 'Henry VIII, six – George IV, one.'

George Radicals trying to whip up more trouble.

Maria On another wall it said 'Bluebeard!'

George Absurd.

Maria Absurd. Yes, there are many things which are absurd. That she shall be Queen is one of them.

George Let's rent you a splendid house in Brighton.

Maria But not near your Pavilion, I expect; and a pension?

George 'The Wounded Party' is your favourite role in the play of your life, isn't it?

Maria I beg your pardon?

George Did you write to her in Brunswick?

Maria Did I what?

George Before that woman came here for the first time all those years ago, did you write and warn her of Lady Jersey?

Maria Those who harbour grudges against Lady Jersey are legion.

George Did you write to Caroline?

117

Maria Have you harboured this grievance all these years?

George And what do you harbour? Do you, for instance, harbour any lingering hopes that I might push through repeals of certain laws?

Maria The repeal of any anti-Catholic laws is a matter for your conscience.

George And is there someone else?

Maria For me?

George Is someone courting you? What about that Marquis?

Maria What Marquis?

George The Marquis de Bellois?

Maria The Marquis de Bellois? He did court me. Poor man.

George Poor? I heard that he was very handsome.

Maria He was the handsomest man in France until he was shot in the face. No. There's no one. I've never betrayed you. When I was twelve, I was sent to an English convent in Paris. My parents came to visit me and took me out. We went to Versailles, where I saw Louis XV pull a chicken apart with his fingers. I laughed, and he was so taken with me he sent the Duc de Soubise to bring me a dish of sugarplums.

George And ever since, you've flirted with royalty.

Maria And royalty has more than flirted with me. During your pursuit of me, I remember vividly the sensation of being glutted with love. When I said come away, I didn't mean come away from the window.

George I have waited all my life to be King.

Maria Here. The portrait of your eye; I don't want you watching me any more.

George I have only watched you because I have been infatuated with you.

Maria Rubbish. You have watches on everyone and anyone. And here. (*Takes out her half of their marriage certificate.*) I annul our marriage. (*Begins to tear it.*) Your Majesty, your most gracious sire, Defender of the Faith, lord of all you survey – with notable exceptions –

George That's enough!

Maria Let me go. I cannot bear it any longer.

Enter McMahon.

McMahon Sir?

Maria Show me out, please, Colonel McMahon. (*Exits.*)

George collects the scraps of marriage certificate.

SCENE FIVE

Westminster Hall. Night.

George Parley.

Caroline Parley.

George Do you enjoy taking the country to the brink?

Caroline I have only defended myself, you should have left me alone.

George When you are left alone, what do you do?

Caroline Whilst you are a saint.

George Openly, with a common foreigner!

Caroline Saint George.

George You have disgraced my family!

Caroline You are the disgrace! You were married already!

George No, that's a –

Caroline Admit it, George, there's no one else near – unless you have one of your incompetent spies hidden.

George It isn't my spies who are incompetent –

Caroline – And what of Charlotte? –

George – It is my lawyers and my politicians! –

Caroline When my daughter and my grandson die together I hear it from a man who happens past my villa!

George You're still trailing that orphan boy about, aren't you?

Caroline You're still trailing that widow about, aren't you? But I am prepared to forgive you –

George Ah, Saint Caroline is with us, now.

Caroline Let he who is without sin.

George Let she who is without shame. How can you assume moral authority over the people?

Caroline I won.

George No. No, no, the Lords were magnanimous in dropping the Bill when it was evident that you have led a life of degradation –

Caroline You exiled me into that life.

George I made you licentious?

Caroline And before you exiled me you locked me away –

George You make it sound as if you were in the Tower –

Caroline I would have become insane –

George Become?

Caroline Both of us need attempt to be generous. Is it true that when at first Mrs Fitzherbert rejected you, you stabbed yourself?

George That is true.

Caroline Stabbed yourself how?

George With a knife. Here. Like so.

Caroline I have no wish to be an obstruction between you. I hope you shall be happy together. I am prepared to speak to her, to acknowledge her in public, to give signals to the nation that she is accepted by the Queen. I shall do everything in my power to –

George She has left me!

Caroline I am truly sorry.

George Why? Why are you sorry? Why do you give a damn about me –

Caroline When you have treated me so abominably?

George No!

Caroline I am not the cause of any of your disappointments –

George Yes!

Caroline No! You were massively in debt and you needed an 'official' wife. I could have made a good 'official' wife except that you didn't want me at all, you didn't even try to want me –

George I tried to make a fist of it –

Caroline A ham fist.

George See! You cannot resist a cheap retort!

Caroline I'd like to make a fist and strike you with it. How could you fail to inform me of the death of our daughter?

George I was melancholy. You hadn't seen her for three years.

Caroline We wrote to one another.

George I was melancholy for a good while. By the time I emerged from my melancholy I assumed that you would have been informed.

Caroline We could have made a fist of it if you had shown me some respect. I first arrived on these shores full of hope –

George Yes, yes –

Caroline Yes, yes, yes! Marrying a mistress? What did you think I would do when I found out that you were already married?

George D'ye know? I don't know. I hadn't thought that far. I was merely getting myself out of a hole. She was never my mistress. I married her, before . . . I love her. Do you love your Italian?

Caroline I am prepared to sue for peace.

George Your terms?

Caroline We are not in a hole, but we are tied to one another.

George Lady Jersey suggested you, you know. What a pair.

Caroline George, in the interests of increasing the sum total of your knowledge of yourself, I have to inform you that I am not how I am with you with anyone else that I have ever met. It is only with you that I am this me. This me is provoked only by you.

George Likewise. What about the Italian? The Baron, Salami or whatever his name is.

Caroline I think you must be referring to the Baron Pergami cited in the Bill against me.

George Are you in love with him?

Caroline I promise that I shall not initiate, perpetuate, or support any action or campaign against you. We shall stage a public reconciliation. I shall conduct my private life in complete seclusion. We shall make no demands on one another beyond the ceremonial.

George Yes.

Caroline Yes?

George Yes, I said yes. You make it all sound very reasonable, wise, just and prudent.

Caroline Yes. But, oh no, oh no; I don't believe you that you agree.

George Of course I don't agree to your ridiculous demands!

Caroline Then what exactly do you propose?

George I swear you shall not be Queen! Do not attempt to attend my Coronation –

Caroline Our Coronation –

George I am the heir, not you. Do not attempt to further whip up the mob – you haven't the moral character to make life and death decisions. Do not cause the army to have to quell their deluded fellow subjects who supported you as the wronged party returning to defend her honour, but who now see you revealed as too flawed to be their example. Go away. Go back to Italy. Your friends shall abandon you. I shall accommodate some of them in my next Government. Your Mr Brougham can be a Member of Parliament if he wishes. He's very ambitious, you know.

Caroline When you've quite finished, I'm still prepared to be reasonable and to sue for peace.

George No, no, no. The you that you claim I bring out in you is the true you. You appear reasonable merely as a ruse.

Caroline Mind that every time you've attacked me, George, I've beaten you off.

George I've never attacked you, I've only ever defended myself and my birthright –

Caroline And I've only ever defended myself –

George And one day my lawyers will not be incompetent! Maybe next time your Mr Brougham will be on my side. I've had a mile of platforms built alongside the route to the Abbey next door. Inside, I've built tiers of benches covered in crimson cloth. And here in the Hall where the banquet shall be taken, the floor shall be covered in blue cloth. Cloth to walk on. My robes are magnificent. A crimson velvet train twenty-seven feet long, ornamented with golden stars, my head-piece topped by ostrich feathers and a heron's plume. The sun reflected off my jewels shall be dazzling. I am secure in the golden castle, your siege has been broken, I was born here, I was the heir, now the King. Tradition shall carry the populace. We saw off the threat from across the Channel – a threat far weightier than that posed by you and yours!

Caroline How has Mrs Fitzherbert ever loved you?

George Rancour, malice and depravity: the three Muses who govern your character.

Caroline Petulance, vengeance, spleen and spite – but four of the defects that contaminate yours.

George Woe the day I married you.

Caroline Rue the day you wronged me. Go to hell with your mother and make a bitch pie!

George I beg your pardon?

Caroline Go to hell with your mother and make a bitch pie!

George Now is laid bare your madness.

Caroline No, now is unleashed my righteousness. I shall see you in the Abbey. (*Exits.*)

Enter McMahon.

McMahon Sir?

George Those Regiments of the army which toasted the Queen.

McMahon Sir?

George Have those Regiments moved out of London until after the Coronation. And the guards for the Coronation, the men on the doors of the Abbey, hand pick them.

Outside Westminster Abbey.
    Off, crowds.

Man (*off*) God save the Queen!

Woman (*off*) God save the King!

The cries are taken up by various others.
    Enter Brougham, Denman.

Brougham Are you sure this is the right gate?

Denman Of course I'm sure.

Brougham You were sure it was Dean's Gate.

Denman And now I am sure it is Poet's Corner.

Woman (*off*) The Queen for ever!

Man (*off*) Here's your wife, Georgie!

Brougham I still say we should enter by the main gate.

Denman We'd never get through.

Brougham You know she's packed her cases?

Denman She'll be moving to a palace, won't she?

Brougham She's also had a carriage made.

Denman And?

Brougham The wheelwright was told to provide extra wheels.

Denman So?

Brougham And the carriage maker was instructed to finish his creation in materials that withstand high temperatures and fierce sunlight. She's returning to Italy.

Denman Then what the hell are we doing here?

Brougham We have to get her inside.

Denman Knowing she plans to abandon us?

Brougham She wants to be crowned –

Denman She's going back to that Italian? –

Brougham We have to get her inside, then we see what happens next. Let's get her inside the Abbey, maintain our momentum –

Denman I'm going to ask her –

Brougham For Heaven's sake don't! We mustn't confront her in view of the crowd.

Denman You should have told me this carriages and Italy business before we got this far.

Brougham We've backed her and we must be seen to continue to back her.

Denman We've backed the wrong horse. We're going to be a laughing –

Brougham Let's just keep the horse going. The race isn't over yet.

> *Enter Caroline, Mariette and Billy.*
> *Caroline takes laudanum.*

Mariette Ma'am?

Caroline I'm alright. Let me take your arm, Billy.

Billy Ouch!

Caroline I'm sorry.

Brougham Make way for the Queen!

Denman Make way for the Queen of England!

127

At the gate, two pugilists and a door-keeper.

Door-Keeper Tickets, please.

Denman I beg your pardon?

Door-Keeper I asked for your tickets, please.

Denman Did you ever hear of a Queen being asked for a ticket before? This is your Queen.

Door-Keeper My orders are without exceptions.

Enter McMahon.

Brougham I am certain your orders did not tell you to refuse admission to your Queen. (*He moves; the way is barred.*)

Door-Keeper Our orders are to admit no person without a ticket.

Denman This is your Queen. She is entitled to admission without such a form.

Caroline Yes, I am your Queen. You must admit me.

Door-Keeper My orders are specific, and I feel bound to obey them.

Brougham I have a ticket.

Door-Keeper Then, my Lord, we shall let you pass upon producing it.

Brougham At last some semblance of sense. (*He enters, then the way is barred.*)

Door-Keeper This ticket admits one person but no more.

Brougham For God's sake, man!

Denman In that case, her Majesty can go in alone?

Brougham She can't go in alone.

Denman Am I to understand that you refuse her Majesty admission?

Door-Keeper We only act in conformity with our orders.

Everyone freezes except Caroline and McMahon.

McMahon Hear the silence? Why has the crowd fallen silent? They all watch this scene. All holding their breath, waiting. All eyes on you, all breath held. Give the signal and those doors are forced open, those guards crushed underfoot, that little man refusing to admit you has not a single bone left unbroken in his body.

At some point, stomach pains and laudanum for Caroline.

The crowd pours in through the gate, all the common herd in their dull garments who have waited three days for a glimpse of brocade, surge in, carried or pushing, screaming, falling. And at all the other gates. And the soldiers shit themselves and fire on the mob, and the mob disarms the soldiers and disembowels them with their own bayonets. All the servile horde's muzzled hate spews out like Satan's bile and killing isn't enough, there shall have to be torture and slashing and biting and mutilation. And when they reach the King his head is torn from his breathing body and impaled on the cross, his blood drips down over Jesus as his mouth works his last. Just cry, 'The Queen! The Queen! Help! Help!' Cry it. Let your revenge against him equal his spite against you. It's not every injured wife who can have a mob act out her revenge. 'The Queen! Help! Help!' Go on.

Enter a Guards Officer. All unfreeze.

Officer Madam, it is my duty to inform your Majesty that there is no place for your Majesty in the Royal Box, or with the Royal Family.

Caroline I am sorry for it. Where's my carriage?

Denman Your Majesty –

Caroline I'd like my carriage.

Officer Your Majesty, I would be happy to escort you.

Brougham I expect you would.

Enter guards.

Caroline Billy, send for Bartolomeo.

Billy Ma'am?

Caroline I am unwell.

Man (*off*) Whore!

Man 2 (*off*) Bedlam Bitch of a Queen!

Mariette Her Majesty's unwell!

Bedlam, off.

SCENE SEVEN

Caroline's bedchamber.
  Caroline in bed. Billy, Mariette, Brougham, Denman, doctors.
  Around the perimeter, George slowly paces.

Doctor It is an obstructed bowel. Nothing passes. Not food nor medicine.

Doctor 2 I have finished bleeding.

Doctor Take laudanum as you require. (*Exit doctors.*)

Caroline Mr Denman. Thank you for everything.

Denman It is not over yet, your Majesty.

Caroline Am I your Majesty? I wasn't crowned, was I? Mr Brougham. This is my will –

Brougham Isn't this premature, your Majesty?

Caroline No. Please execute it. I wish to be buried in Brunswick. I am sorry your tenure as the Queen's Attorney General has been truncated. You shall have a period in the doldrums, but then I am reliably informed you shall have a new patron. You deserve advancement. You have a brilliant mind.

Brougham Thank you, your Majesty.

Mariette Ma'am. Lord Malmesbury is here.

Caroline Is he? He's very welcome.

Exit Denman and Brougham.
Enter Malmesbury.

Malmesbury Ma'am, what do the doctors say?

Caroline They avoid my eye, that is enough.

Malmesbury Shall I bring other doctors?

Caroline Thank you, but no. It is fitting you are here tonight, you who brought me here.

Malmesbury I failed to protect you though, Ma'am.

Caroline What could you have done?

Malmesbury Perhaps if earlier someone had intervened –

Caroline Tell me, when you came to Brunswick to bring me here, did you think I was suitable?

Malmesbury Yes, Ma'am.

Caroline Don't lie to me tonight.

Malmesbury I had certain reservations about the match, Ma'am. I have to inform you, Ma'am, that despite great reservations, my conscience and duty made me vote in the House in favour of your being stripped of your title. I wanted you to know that.

Caroline You have always been a man of principle.

Malmesbury You are too kind, Ma'am.

Caroline I know you are not against me personally.

Malmesbury You may be assured of that.

Caroline And you lost.

Malmesbury We all lost, Ma'am, in my opinion.

Caroline Thank you for coming to see me.

Malmesbury Your humble servant. (*Exits.*)

Malmesbury approaches George, who stops pacing. A mute exchange. Exit Malmesbury. George recommences his slow pacing.

Caroline Well, Mariette, you may return to Brunswick very soon. We shall have been a long time away. I know you haven't always approved –

Mariette Ma'am, I –

Caroline Call me Caroline. Call me once by my name.

Mariette I cannot.

Caroline Billy won't tell anyone.

Billy No.

Mariette Shall I just say your name, your name on its own?

Caroline No. Preface it with 'goodnight'.

Mariette Goodnight, Caroline. (*Exits.*)

Caroline Billy boy. My will leaves everything to you, bar a pension for Mariette and another for Lady Jersey.
I want you to promise me that you shall make over the deeds of the Villa to Bartolomeo.

Billy I promise.

Caroline On my headstone I wish inscribed: 'Here lies Caroline, the injured Queen of England.'

Billy Yes.

Caroline Let me look at you. You are quite easily the best Englishman I have ever met. Oh, Billy. I hope you fall in love at least once in your lifetime. You won't have any trouble wooing the ladies but I do hope you fall in love.

Billy I am in love.

Caroline Really? Who is –

Billy I love you.

Caroline Oh, Billy. That's a lovely thing to say. Can you learn something for me?

Billy What?

Caroline I want you to be able to repeat this to Bartolomeo.

Billy Yes.

Caroline Tell him: I am sorry –

Billy I am sorry.

Caroline I have had to go on somewhere else.

Billy I have had to go on somewhere else.

Caroline We shall meet there.

Billy We shall meet there.

Caroline Repeat it thus far.

Billy I am sorry. I have had to go on somewhere else. We shall meet there.

Caroline Oh Billy. Oh Billy. Oh Billy.

Billy Tell me more. There is more. There must be more.

Caroline More?

Billy Yes.

Caroline Tell him: Oh Bartolomeo – I meant to return – I truly did – I had to I shouldn't have – I shouldn't have you were right – what a futile – I should have stayed – look what I had!

Billy Quiet. I'll get some laudanum.

He turns away. She watches him. She dies.

Here. What? Then? Just then?

Enter Brougham, Denman, Mariette, doctors, Malmesbury.

I turned away!

Doctor Ten twenty-five p.m.

Malmesbury I shall let it be known.